THE HAPPIEST
DOG
ON THE BLOCK

THE HAPPIEST DOG ON THE BLOCK

CANINE **ENRICHMENT ACTIVITIES** TO KEEP YOUR PET **YOUNG** AND **HEALTHY**

❧ TAYLOR FINTON ❧

CASTLE POINT BOOKS

NEW YORK

www.castlepointbooks.com

The Castle Point Books trademark is owned by Castle Point Publishing, LLC.
Castle Point books are published and distributed by St. Martin's Publishing Group.

ISBN 978-1-250-34723-7 (trade paperback)
ISBN 978-1-250-34724-4 (ebook)

Design by Joanna Williams

Photography by Taylor Finton except cover photo and pages 9, 12, 19 (bottom), 20, 36, 73, 84, 88, 98, 101, 104, 106, 109–11, 117–18, 120, 123, 125, 127–8, 134–5, 138, 144, 150, 153, 157–8, 162, 164, 167, 171–2, 175–6, and 178–9 used under license from Shutterstock

Edited by Jennifer Leight

Our books may be purchased in bulk for promotional, educational, or business use.
Please contact your local bookseller or the Macmillan Corporate and Premium Sales Department at 1-800-221-7945, extension 5442, or by email at MacmillanSpecialMarkets@macmillan.com.

First Edition: 2024

10 9 8 7 6 5 4 3 2 1

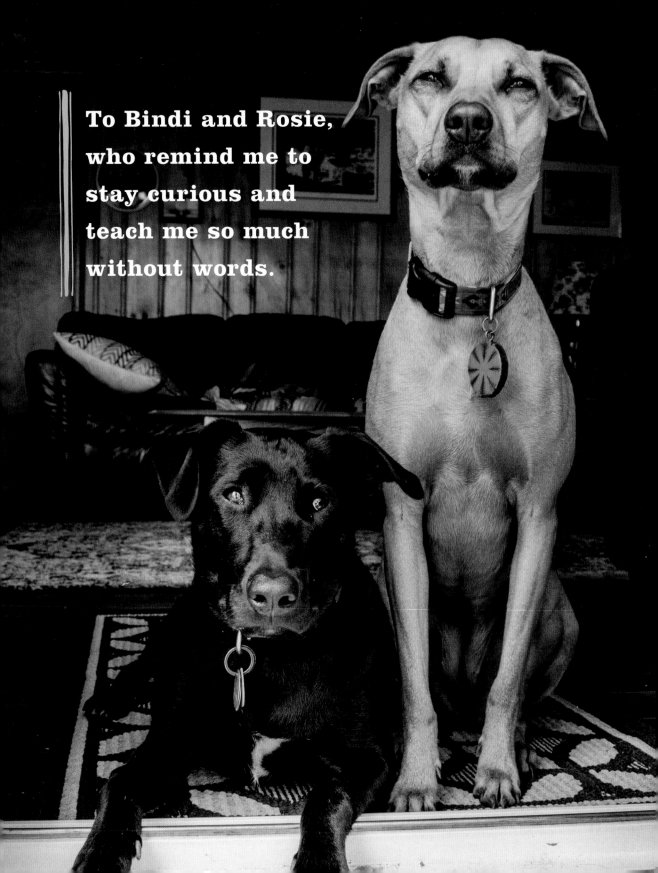

To Bindi and Rosie, who remind me to stay curious and teach me so much without words.

Contents

Welcome

Having an *aha* moment is an amazing feeling! You know what I'm talking about—the moment when you learn something new and suddenly everything just *clicks*. My aha moment came in 2018 when my husband and I adopted not one but two rescue puppies. Our dogs, Bindi and Rosie, opened up our world and wriggled their way into our hearts and homes (as most dogs do!). With them full of spunk and puppy energy, I soon found myself looking for ways to keep them as happy and as healthy as I could.

I love to read, so I dove into books, articles, and studies to learn more about my canine companions. All the while, I happily stuffed feeder toys, gave the puppies food puzzles, and let them sniff at their favorite walk spots—not knowing much about *why* the dogs loved these things but happy to see the positive connection.

Then I stumbled upon the term *enrichment*. It helped me to understand why my dogs responded better to certain choices and the next steps I could take to keep toys and activities engaging for them. It helped me see what dogs need to be at their best—physically, socially, emotionally, and cognitively.

Eager to share enrichment with fellow dog lovers, I started a blog and social media accounts that swiftly became an active community. What a beautiful thing to see positive outcomes for dogs and their owners—a celebration of lots of aha moments!

Discovering enrichment has been one of the most fulfilling experiences of my life. Bindi and Rosie are appreciative as well. I've had the pleasure of working with and learning from some of the best enrichment brands, trainers, and advocates. Now I'm excited to bring enrichment to you in ways that are easy to understand, implement, and adapt for your dog's needs.

So if you're a loving pet parent who just wants to learn a little more about how to have happier, healthier dogs, you've come to the right place. Welcome to the enrichment community. Nothing fancy required. Have fun, be creative, and watch your dog thrive and your relationship with your dog blossom! Enrichment's purpose is happiness, which will no doubt reflect back to you once you see it in your dog.

—Taylor Finton
Bindisbucketlist.com

The Secret to Happy Dogs

Of all the gifts we give our dogs—from the best food and the most comfortable bed to tons of toys and praise—the gift our pups may appreciate most is giving them the chance to be dogs in healthy ways. That's the heart of enrichment.

Anything from letting your dog have extra time to sniff on a walk to treating your pooch to a food stuffer and even allowing them to chase bubbles can be considered enrichment. The goal is simply to provide activities that encourage dogs to indulge in natural behaviors (think: sniffing, foraging, playing, shredding, licking, chasing, and chewing) through positive outlets (read: not destroying any furniture or neighbor relationships).

Lots of enrichment activities provide at least a little physical activity, but the most powerful outcomes result from mental exercise. Working your dog's brain with fun experiences and sensory challenges lessens hyperactivity, lowers stress, deters destructive behavior, and makes your dog overall happier and healthier. Isn't that what we're all trying to do for our furry companions?

To show you how easy it can be, you'll find more than fifty step-by-step enrichment ideas in a wide variety of categories throughout this book. You're sure to find activities you and your dog will love! But first, it helps to understand how enrichment works and how to match activities to your dog.

THE ABCDs OF ENRICHMENT

One of the most amazing aspects of enrichment is how it works in so many different ways to benefit our dogs. It goes much deeper than keeping them busy. Enrichment stimulates their senses to activate positive physical effects in the body,

increases the bond between you and your pet, relieves pent-up stress through choice, and helps dogs decompress through physical and emotional release.

Activation

Enrichment activities can activate pleasure centers in your dog's brain and balance hormones. Healthy mental challenges can tame the stress hormone cortisol while amping up endorphins and dopamine. You know endorphins as that "runner's high" in humans—it's known to boost immunity and reduce anxiety. Dopamine can help learning, motivation, and attention—hello, Good Boy.

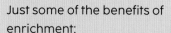

Enriched Dogs Are Happy Dogs

Just some of the benefits of enrichment:

- Activates the pleasure centers of your dog's brain
- Provides mental stimulation
- Alleviates boredom
- Promotes calmness
- Strengthens the bond between you and your pet
- Can be used as positive reinforcement
- Can be used to help mitigate fear, anxiety, and stress (sometimes referred to as FAS spectrum)

Bond

On a simple level, your dog will be grateful to you for providing fun activities that let a dog be a dog. But consider that enrichment activities can also help release oxytocin, the bonding chemical—encouraging chill time with you and other human and furry family members.

Choice

From when we wake up to what we eat and how we dress, humans make thousands of choices each day, whether we consciously realize it or not. But what about our canine companions? When it comes to free choice, our dogs' outlets are limited. Much of their decision-making is taken over by us in their day-to-day lives. Offering safe choices through enrichment is a great way to provide stress relief and improve your dog's well-being. It can also help us learn individual preferences so we can bring our dogs greater joy.

Decompression

Know how you get home from a crazy-busy day and need to find some release? Dogs need that decompression too. Enrichment activities can guide them into a calm, balanced state of mind by releasing serotonin into their brain. Pay attention to the activities that center them and lower stress levels. While preference can vary by dog, sniffing activities like sniffari walks (page 35) often work well to give your dog a sigh of relief—and walks are good for your state of mind as well.

Long Live Enrichment

A study published in *Neurobiology of Aging* found that enrichment activities may slow the aging process in the canine brain. Older dogs who participated in enrichment activities had about 18 percent more neurons in a certain area of the brain compared to older dogs who were not stimulated with enrichment activities. Along with helping to maintain cognitive function, enrichment activities also connect dogs to their people more closely. Vets point to that bond as an advantage in discovering health issues quickly, leading to early detection and treatment.

BUSTING ENRICHMENT MYTHS

With so many benefits, why don't we jump into enrichment the moment we bring our dogs into our homes? Some common but untrue ideas can hang us up before we even give enrichment activities a try.

Myth: Dogs just want your love

I mean, yes . . . but also no. As much as we humans want to love and be loved, we also know that love alone doesn't fully sustain all of our needs. We need opportunities to build

What Dogs Need

You may be familiar with Maslow's hierarchy of needs (cue the flashbacks to high school psychology class!). But what does this look like when it comes to our dogs? While we can all agree that we're very different from our dogs, many of Maslow's human tiers mirror the same hierarchy of needs reflected in our canine companions. Here's my take on Maslow's hierarchy when it comes to our pet dogs.

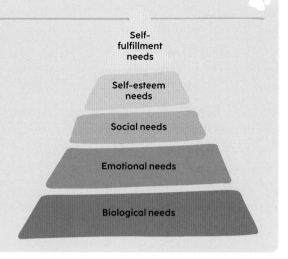

Self-fulfillment needs

Self-esteem needs

Social needs

Emotional needs

Biological needs

mastery and self-confidence; ways to exercise curiosity, freedom, and choice; chances to learn, grow, and find purpose. Happy, healthy dogs need satisfaction in these areas too!

So, yes, of course, enrichment is a fantastic way to show our love for our pets. But it goes a lot deeper. With cognitive and physical benefits, happiness-inducing qualities, stress-relieving power, and so much more, enrichment is one of the best gifts that we can give any animal in our care.

Myth: Enrichment is entirely food-based

This food focus is possibly one of the biggest misconceptions about enrichment, but it's easy to see how the limiting myth came about. After all, most dogs tend to be extremely food-motivated and outwardly show us their happiness over food and treats. Even hearing the door to the treat cupboard opening can lead to a barrage of happy feet, wagging tails, and drooling lips. Pet owners see instant gratification as we watch food-motivated dogs dig into a fun enrichment treat, whereas enjoyment of other enrichment types can be harder or slower to observe. As a result, a dog's subtle reaction can sometimes be construed as indifference or dislike in comparison to the big, elaborate displays of happiness often seen with food.

But food is far from the only way to offer enrichment! You may be missing out on tons of other easy and fun nonfood ways to create enjoyment and healthy challenge for your dog—toys like flirt poles to chase, scent games to play, even music to engage. In the end, you may discover that your dog's favorite activity isn't what you assumed—and doesn't require a super-stocked treat cabinet.

Myth: Allowing dogs to follow instincts like chewing will just encourage bad behavior

Behaviors like chewing and chasing aren't bad in dogs; they're natural. But we don't want those instincts expressed in ways that are destructive or dangerous. So redirection makes perfect sense! Redirection lets your dog know what's acceptable to chew (a treat or food stuffer, not your shoes or furniture) and what's acceptable to chase (a ball or flirt pole, not your cat). When you provide fun outlets, you'll encourage fulfillment, not frustration. Not convinced? A study in *Applied Animal Behaviour Science* showed that introducing enrichment to dogs decreased their chewing of furniture by 80 percent. Researchers concluded that appropriate enrichment can help to prevent undesirable behaviors and reinforce positive ones.

Myth: Enrichment must be elaborate to be effective

Enrichment offerings don't need to be difficult; they need to be fun! Owners sometimes get overly caught up in seeking over-the-top challenges and stimulation for their dog and miss their pup's cues that a game is not as fun as humanly assumed. Watch for signs of frustration: excessive barking at the toy or activity, pacing, panting, and walking away.

Often, the simplest games are the most enjoyable and engaging for dogs. Let's not measure the quality of enrichment by the time or money invested. Instead, let's focus on our dogs' overall joy with the game, toy, experience, or interaction. They will let us know in their own way.

Myth: Enrichment is expensive

While enrichment toy marketing absolutely skyrocketed during the pandemic, you don't have to break the bank to create brain games and enjoyment. Contrary to popular belief, enrichment can be a very inexpensive way

Through a Dog's Eyes

Try considering enrichment activities from different lenses to help understand what your dog is enjoying and where you could explore more. Here are some of the most common ways to look at enrichment categories:

- **By sense:** sight, sound, touch, taste, scent
- **By need fulfilled:** environmental, sensory, cognitive, social, physical, nutritional, occupational
- **By general type of activity:** walking/hiking, solving puzzles, foraging, sniffing, water play

to show love for your dog. You just need to know where to look for creative, dog-friendly supplies. Items you probably already have on hand—like old towels, cardboard boxes, and egg cartons—can work wonders as enrichment experiences. The cost can be little to nothing!

While big, elaborate puzzles and games can be exciting, so can a simple treat puzzle made from an ordinary towel (known as a snuffle mat) or a classic rubber food-stuffer toy (KONG is a popular brand name) given at dinnertime. Just because your enrichment may not be as fancy as someone else's doesn't mean that it's ineffective or wrong.

START HERE FOR A HAPPY DOG

Part of the beauty of enrichment is that it's a wide open space, not a set formula. It's exciting to see so many enrichment ideas being shared through books, training sessions, and social media. But that also brings up a dilemma: Where do you start? Let the three pillars of enrichment be your guide!

1. Individual Preference

It may sound simple, but sometimes we overlook an essential question. Ask yourself, *What does my dog enjoy? How can I build more of that into their routine?* Each dog has distinct likes—from specific toys to social versus isolated play style. Having a grasp on what your dog gravitates toward is a great starting point. So keep what you know so far about your dog in mind.

Then go with the try-and-see approach. Be patient and remember to have fun as you discover what makes your dog tick. One glaring example: you may just find that your dog isn't food-motivated at all (which is much more common than people think). As you test enrichment experiences that seem like a match for your dog, watch their reaction. It will get easier and easier to pinpoint what games, activities, and enrichment pairings they'll enjoy best. Like us, dogs have individual preferences. When you can identify preferences, you may start to see deeper patterns of what brings your dog joy.

2. Variety & Novelty

Variety and novelty are both key aspects to include in enrichment. They keep activities exciting and fun. Think about it this way: as kids, many of us looked forward to

Ask yourself: Would your dog prefer food-based enrichment or play-based enrichment?

exchanging valentines or celebrating a birthday with a party. These activities were special because they were novel experiences, which means that they weren't something that we received every single day. If these events were part of the daily routine, it might seem fantastic *at first.* But the magic would quickly be lost.

Mixing up enrichment experiences—whether toys, treats, or activities—helps keep the magic alive for your dog. At least one study also points to variety in your dog's routine as a way to decrease stress. Dogs staying in a kennel showed less physical and behavioral stress when varied music was played over the course of 5 days. Although certain types of music initially had a stronger calming effect, the effect seemed to wear off as time went on. Mixing up the music brought back the de-stressing power. If music enrichment can fall into a rut, there's no reason to think the same isn't true for all kinds of enrichment. Dogs can get bored, just like us!

3. Sense of Choice

Here's that encouragement again to provide choice! Remember that a sense of choice in

enrichment is a pivotal part of why it's so enjoyable for dogs. As a result, offering enrichment options (when safe to do so) can be extremely rewarding and beneficial for dogs. You can try out the power of choice by giving your dog a few toy choices at

Learn the Terms

As you join the enrichment circle, you may come across some unfamiliar terms or new uses for terms. Here are a few to start you off.

Biological fulfillment: This term covers all the ways we meet our dogs' innate needs—from food and shelter to genetic and instinctual needs as well (for example, sniffing, chasing, chewing, digging, licking). You'll begin to see how enrichment fits right in.

Contrafreeloading: It's a fancy way to describe the behavior seen when an animal is given a choice between free food and food that requires effort. Perhaps surprisingly, they tend to choose the food that requires effort. What's the deal? Chalk it up to thrill seeking. Our dogs enjoy the anticipation of receiving the food more than obtaining the actual food itself. Learn more on page 49.

Decompression: Whether we're talking about airplane cabins, scuba diving, or simply coming home at the end of a long day, decompression is the release of pressure. After trying so hard to please, dogs need it too! Many enrichment activities are designed with decompression in mind, allowing our dogs to find a calm headspace.

Foraging: While your mind may jump to forests and mushrooms, you'll also find this term connected to canine enrichment. It's simply the act of searching for and gathering resources—namely, food. Historically, canines in the wild would have had plenty of foraging opportunities. Many dogs still feel the instinctual pull. Fortunately, there are many ways that we can mimic foraging activities through enrichment. Get started on page 23!

Positive outlet: In enrichment, a positive outlet is a game or activity that allows your dog the opportunity to have a constructive release of energy or behavior. For example, creating a dig pit (like on pages 99-101) allows your dog to have fun and blow off steam while simultaneously keeping him out of your flower bed.

Snuffle: This may simply describe a sniffing sound, but it's often used as a slang term for sniffing during enrichment activities. Consider: *snuffle* mats—those squares of material with loops in which to hide food. You'll learn how to create snuffle activities starting on page 25.

Stuffable toys: These wonders are designed for stuffing with food as an enrichment treat. They come in a wide variety of options to suit dogs of every shape and size. Tasty Treats & Stuffers, starting on page 55, offers lots of stuffing ideas that are doable for you and delicious and nutritious for your dog.

playtime, setting up a taste test on a lick mat, or allowing your dog to pick the sniff stops on a walk. Be careful to watch out for choice overload. Just as in our own lives, too many choices for dogs may overwhelm them. Sometimes, less is more.

Bring It All Together 1-2-3

Once you have a grasp on these three pillars, you're able to make enrichment-based decisions and create rewarding routines that focus on your dog as an individual. Here's an example of how to use the plan:

1. ID a form of enrichment your dog enjoys.

My dog really likes sniffing activities.

2. Provide different variations to keep things novel and interesting.

I allow my dog to spend time walking and sniffing on a long leash and offer a variety of snuffle mats and puzzles as part of our routine.

3. Offer other outlets to provide a sense of choice.

Even though sniffing ranks highest, I still offer fetch, stuffable toys, and other enrichment activities to which my dog responds positively.

Watch for your dog's reactions and modify your plan when you notice . . .

- Your dog is getting frustrated.
- Your dog is losing interest.
- Your dog has mastered the activity.

You can also modify enrichment activity plans to account for age and any special needs (from short-term injuries to blindness or paralysis). You'll find lots of creative ways to adapt activities for your dog throughout the activity chapters and answers to questions about engaging dogs with special challenges, starting on page 178.

READY, SET, ENRICH!

The chapters that follow are set up by general type of activity, so you can jump in simply by scanning for what your dog enjoys or needs—whether that's sniffing and foraging fun, food motivation, chase games, bonding time with you or another dog, or a little environmental stimulation. Each activity is also highlighted with key categories such as indoor versus outdoor, quick, good for sensitive dogs, uses recycled materials, and works well for multiple dogs. You'll know what to expect at a glance. But your best resource may be the Enrichment Match Game (pages 185–191), a full chart of every idea in the book and how it delivers across many categories.

So dig in and give your dog the simple yet powerful gift of enrichment. You'll see an immediate change in your pup's behavior, form a stronger bond with your four-legged companion, and get your vet's nods of approval!

Sniffing & Foraging Fun

Sniffing and foraging are natural canine tendences and activities that release dopamine, the happy brain chemical, in your dog. Fortunately, your dog can fulfill these needs in ways you'll both love (read: no trash can cleanup and your plants survive). Get ready to unleash sniffing satisfaction and foraging adventures for a calmer household!

Bite-size dry treats of any kind work well in a snuffle mat. You can also expand the adventure with dog-friendly veggies or fruits such as chopped carrots, apples, green beans, or broccoli or pup-smart herbs such as chopped parsley or mint.

TIP

Snuffle Snack Break

Good for Sensitive Dogs | Indoor | Quick Setup | Soothing

While you don't need to invest tons of money in enrichment toys, a snuffle mat is a smart, small purchase that pays back quickly in dog decompression. This type of mat is specifically designed to entice dogs into sniffing and foraging when you hide treats within the spaces of its fleece strips. So simple yet so rewarding for your pup!

WHAT YOU'LL NEED

- **Dry treats of choice**
- **Snuffle mat**

SNUFFLE SCIENCE

That happy dog reaction you see when you bring out the snuffle mat may last longer than you realize. A study on olfactory behavior in pet dogs found that letting them engage in sniffing behaviors regularly made them more optimistic. No, we can't ask dogs if their bowl is half-empty or half-full, but researchers can judge by how dogs approach unfamiliar stimuli.

STEP BY STEP

1. Sprinkle treats into the spaces and folds of the snuffle mat with a food scoop or simply your hands.

2. Use your hands to ensure the treats are buried in the mat and the strips are fluffed up for more foraging challenge.

3. Invite your dog to sniff and seek.

KEEP IT CLEAN

- Wash your snuffle mat regularly to avoid bacteria buildup. I try to wash mine at least once a week, but cleaning needs can vary based on the ingredients used and how often you use the mat.
- Before putting your mat in the wash, shake it out and use your fingers to comb through any bits your dog may have left behind.
- Most snuffle mats are machine washable on a delicate low-heat cycle with a mild detergent.
- Follow with a tumble dry on low heat, or hang to air-dry.
- If you purchase a snuffle mat from a vendor, ask for cleaning tips and tricks.

You can use any towels, but thick, bulky towels are harder to roll.

TIP

Stingray Snuffle Puzzle

Good for Sensitive Dogs | Indoor | Sensory Experience | Uses Recycled Items

You can buy or make snuffle mats with fleece strips that create a space in which to hide treats. But you can also transform ordinary towels into snuffle challenges. Let's face it, we all have a stockpile of spares in the back of the linen closet, and they're so dang easy to throw in the laundry! The hidden treats encourage nose work and natural foraging tendencies.

WHAT YOU'LL NEED

- **1 large towel**
- **Dry treats of choice**
- **1 hand towel**

LOVE FOR SNUFFLES

- **Initiate sniffing and foraging centers of the brain, which are pleasurable for dogs**
- **Alleviate stress**
- **Offer mental stimulation**
- **Encourage slower (healthier) eating habits**
- **Especially good for senior, fearful, and nervous dogs, and dogs on restricted exercise**

STEP BY STEP

1. Spread the large towel out flat.

2. Sprinkle the dry treats all over the towel.

3. Roll up each side of your towel, meeting in the middle.

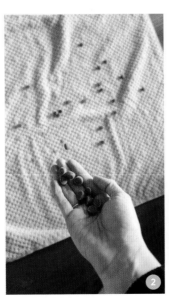

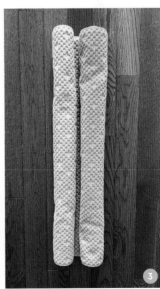

THE HAPPIEST DOG ON THE BLOCK

4. Flip the towel over so that the rolls are now on the bottom. Fold one end up about a third of the way over the rolls.

5. Flip over once more. The folded side should be facing the bottom now.

6. Unroll the ends farthest from the folded section. Spread this section until you've reached your desired width.

7. To start the tail, lay the hand towel out flat. Sprinkle on additional treats, if desired.

8. Using your finger to hold down a corner, roll the short side from the corner until the entire towel comes into one roll.

9. Place the rolled towel tail under the stingray body. The tip of the tail should be where your finger was placed.

10. Add two treats as eyes and serve.

ADAPT FOR YOUR DOG

- Never be afraid to offer help should your dog need it. It may take some dogs a moment to figure out the game the first time or two.

- If your dog likes to pick up towels and shake them, try placing a weighted toy or two in the middle of the puzzle to ground it and create a little more challenge.

Towel Tornado

Good for All Ages | Indoor | Quick Setup | Uses Recycled Items

You can create snuffle puzzles for your canine companion in so many ways. If you're not ready to master the Stingray Snuffle Puzzle, or you're looking for something that can be set up in under 5 minutes, a tornado is what you need to calm your dog. The Towel Tornado is one of the easiest towel snuffle variations to set up, and it works just as well as more complex configurations!

WHAT YOU'LL NEED

- **1 large towel**
- **Dry treats of choice**

SNUFFLES AS SOLUTIONS

Rainy day or exercise restrictions? Snuffles—both ready-to-go mats and DIY puzzles—are great for providing a mental workout for dogs who are stuck inside or on restricted exercise. They offer a safe and effective way for dogs to expend their energy and stay mentally engaged, even when they can't go for a walk or run.

STEP BY STEP

1. Spread the towel out flat.

2. Sprinkle the dry treats all over the towel.

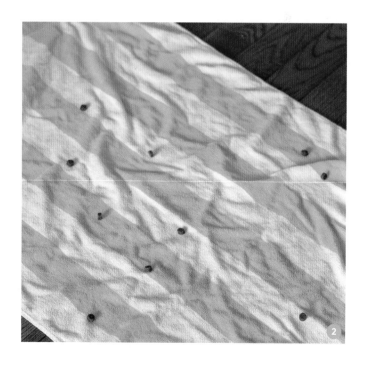

3. With your hand like a claw, grab the center of the towel and turn the section you've grabbed clockwise. The towel should come together, forming a little tornado of crevices. These little folds help hide the treats.

4. Tuck in any visible treats and serve.

ADAPT FOR YOUR DOG

- When increasing the difficulty, aim to make your dog think, not fail. Place treats to be hidden but accessible so that the puzzle does not cause frustration.

- Does your dog take off with the towel? Try folding it up and placing it inside a shallow laundry basket.

Set Snuffle Boundaries

Wondering whether giving your dog towel puzzles will make them fixate on towels? When towel challenges are introduced correctly, not at all!

Dogs are masters in reading and deciphering the cues that we give them. If your dog suddenly begins seeking out towels (not meant to be dog toys!) around your home, take a look at your pattern of serving towel puzzles. Are you leaving the towel out on the floor once the game is completed? Are you using sticky treats, leaving food residue on the towels?

To help your dog know the difference between acceptable towel puzzles and the fancier human-designated supply, take these steps:

Set an end. Always remove the towel once the game is complete. Your dog will learn that you make the towel come and go, you initiate this kind of play, and the game is complete once the treats are found. Similarly, put store-bought snuffle mats away once your dog is finished foraging to discourage any rough play with the mat.

Monitor play. Only let your dog interact with a snuffle towel or mat when you're around to watch your dog use it. Certain dogs, when finished foraging, will try to tear at the towel or mat's fleece pieces. Your supervision will stop this behavior and ensure that your snuffle lasts more than a few servings.

Jump in, as needed. Always intervene if you see that your dog is frustrated and/or not understanding the activity. Redirect any non-foraging behaviors (such as biting the towel or pulling at a mat's fleece as opposed to sniffing through the folds) and reward your pup when they're engaging in the game correctly.

Aside from protecting the good linens, creating boundaries ensures your dog gets the most out of snuffle activity.

TIP

Sniffy walks can be enjoyed off leash in secure areas and with dogs safe to do so. No matter the situation, it's a good idea to bring along a standard (4- to 6-foot) leash for better control in a pinch.

Sniffari Adventure

Energy Outlet | Good for You Too | Outdoor | Works Well for Multiple Dogs

Whether you call it a sniffari, sniffy walk, or decompression walk, the type of walk that provides space for your dog's exploration—not constant "point A to point B"—is extremely beneficial for your pooch. Dogs actually decompress through their nose. Sniffy walks also allow freedom of movement and a sense of choice for our furry companions in a safe way.

WHAT YOU'LL NEED

- **Long line/lead**
- **Harness that allows comfortable movement**
- **Safe space away from hustle and bustle**

LOVE FOR SNIFFARIS

- **Release pressure**
- **Lower pulse through sniffing decompression**
- **Offer mental and sensory stimulation**
- **Get you both out for fresh air**
- **Easy to welcome a human and/or canine companion**

STEP BY STEP

1. Gather your gear. Keep in mind that BioThane long lines are much easier to clean as opposed to long lines made of fabric. A very sturdy Flexi leash also does the trick if you're going for a hike where there are lots of roots, trees, or water. This way, your line is not dragging on the ground.

A harness alleviates any tension between the long line and neck. Check for a fit that allows shoulder movement.

2. Find your place. Walk in a space that allows your dog the freedom to move, sniff, and explore at will. Think: empty (or at least, less-crowded) green space. This could be a park, soccer field, trail, or beach.

3. Breathe and watch your dog be a dog! Once you've reached your intended area, let the line go slack and allow your dog to wander. Watch where their nose takes them. Where do they choose to explore, and what's their body language telling you? Part of the beauty of sniffaris is the freedom of choice they give our dogs to partake in natural dog behaviors (such as sniffing, chasing, chewing) in a positive way.

TIP

A backyard mint garden is a great space for scatter feeding. Your dog can safely ingest mint leaves, so both their breath and fur will smell fresh after their snuffling adventure!

Scatter Feeding

Food Motivation | Good for Sensitive Dogs | Outdoor | Quick Setup

Don't be afraid to get wild with snuffle challenges! You can take the idea of hiding dry treats and expand the play into nature's spaces versus the spaces of a snuffle mat or folded towel. Often called scatter feeding, "feeding the chickens" is what our household lovingly calls it. With no toys required, it's extremely easy to toss together (pun intended!) in a pinch.

WHAT YOU'LL NEED

- **Space with lush grass or foliage**
- **Dry treats of choice**

SCATTER SCIENCE

While scatter feeding can be fun in a group, one study found that dogs typically eat faster when buddies are present. Consider keeping it a solo experience if you want your dog to take in the full calming effects of a scatter feed. Although there are no hard rules, you'll want to think about your desired outcome when setting up your pooch.

STEP BY STEP

1. Pick your location. For optimal snuffling opportunities, seek a space with long grass that offers lots of hidden places for treats to fall. Always ensure that the space you've chosen is free of pesticides or lawn treatments that may be harmful to your dog.

2. Sprinkle treats across the space, allowing them to fall into the grassy maze below.

3. Allow your dog to sniff and forage through the space at their own pace.

Never Be Afraid to Offer Help

While scatter feeding may seem simple for our dogs to understand, some pups may require guidance and reassurance. Offering help during enrichment is never a bad thing (in fact, quite the opposite!). Your guidance can help your dog learn how to interact with and get the most benefit from these types of foraging activities.

Party Cup Scent Seek

Indoor or Outdoor | Cognitive Challenge | Sensory Experience

You can host a scent game for your dog with items you probably already have on hand. Grab some party cups from your pantry stash and start singing "I fill you up" as you pull out treats and imagine the maze you'll set up. In cold or rainy weather, you can keep the fun in your living room. In nice weather, you can take it outdoors. Make the scent trail short or long, depending on your needs and your dog's interest.

WHAT YOU'LL NEED

- **Treats of any kind— from bite-size biscuits or dehydrated green beans to bits of rotisserie chicken**
- **Plastic party cups**

STEP BY STEP

1. Place treats around your house or yard, covering them with party cups as you go.

2. For an added challenge, set up some cups with nothing underneath. This will encourage your dog to follow their nose to find their treats instead of just looking for the cups.

3. Release the hound and watch your dog go to work with their nose.

Success with Sensitive Dogs

If your dog is sensitive to sounds and movements, keep at least the first few rounds on carpet. Light plastic party cups move with ease on hardwood and tile and make a loud sound when toppling on these surfaces. While this isn't a problem for some dogs, it may be a little scary for others who are skittish. Always anticipate and adjust for what your dog needs.

TIP Choose the treats based on the game location. For indoors, I tend to use dry treats to keep it simple and clean. For outdoors, I lean toward something high-value like rotisserie chicken or sardines to keep the dogs engaged in a more distracting setting.

SCENTS THAT MAKE SENSE

For dogs who are less treat-inclined, try simply scents.

- Start by drilling or punching holes into the top of small glass canning jars.
- Place dog-friendly herbs and spices (clove is one good choice) into the jars, seal the lids, and hide the jars under the cups.

- To amp it up, place a few drops of a dog-safe scent oil (such as birch, anise, or even deer or quail) on a cotton swab, then place it in the jar using plastic gloves.
- Always research what is safe for pups.

Scentsory Box

Good for Puppies | Good for Older Dogs | Sensory Experience | Uses Recycled Items

Your dog's nose is one of the ways they "see" the world. While any dog can benefit from this enrichment activity, it's particularly good for puppies, older dogs, or dogs who may not be able to go on as many adventures as they used to. Through scents, you'll essentially be bringing new and exciting experiences from out in the wild to your dog right at home. Just imagine all the places he'll go!

WHAT YOU'LL NEED

- 1 tote bag
- Towels, blankets, or items of clothing (for example, a sweater, jeans, mittens)
- 1 box or laundry basket

LOVE FOR SCENTS

While it sometimes seems like dogs' noses are attracted to just about *everything*, our canine companions may have scent preferences, according to researchers. Here are some of the scents that dogs seek out the most:

- **Blackberries**
- **Blueberries**
- **Lavender**
- **Mint**
- **Roses**

STEP BY STEP

1. Brainstorm some different locations that contain scents that may be new or at least unusual to your dog—for example, farms, fields, the zoo, a friend's house.

2. The next time you're out and about, take your tote bag with you to bring home certain items your dog might find interesting. Going on a hike? Pick up some pinecones, a stick, or even some dry leaves. Visiting a

Sniff Sniff, Hooray!

After a long day outside, returning home to your dog's warm welcome is one of the best feelings in the world. You may not realize it, but those moments when your furry friend excitedly sniffs you at the door are an incredible display of olfactory behavior. With each twitch of the nose, your dog is decoding their environment. According to studies, a dog's sense of smell is a whopping ten thousand to one hundred thousand times stronger than that of a human!

farm? Think about hay, your boots with dried mud, and the sweater you wore. Always be mindful of your environment, and only take things when safe and permissible to do so.

3. Place these items into a box or laundry basket, then allow your dog to sniff through them.

> **Think about bringing in unique items and smells as providing your dog with a newspaper or novel; with each twitch of the nose, your dog is flipping the page to a new chapter of discovery. Exposure to new scents is highly beneficial for dogs' brains.**

TIP

Egg-cellent Carton Game

Good for All Ages | Quick Setup | Shredding Outlet | Uses Recycled Items

All you need for this enrichment game is an empty egg carton and some treats, but you can add in crinkly paper for more stimulation. It's simple fun that allows your dog to tap into their foraging instincts to obtain the treats. Watch how their nose goes wild as they begin to dig in! Bonus: allowable carton shredding at the end of the hunt.

WHAT YOU'LL NEED

- **Dry treats of choice**
- **Empty egg carton**
- **Crinkly brown paper (such as packing paper or a paper bag)**

LOVE FOR SNIFFING + SHREDDING

- **The act of sniffing provides calm mental stimulation.**
- **Sniffing engages but at the same time lowers pulse rate.**
- **Shredding offers physical release to help relaxation.**

STEP BY STEP

1. Sprinkle the dry treats inside the segments of the egg carton.

2. If using the crinkly brown paper, cut or tear it into strips. Scrunch the pieces of paper and place them over the treats in the egg carton.

3. Close the egg carton and serve.

4. Let your dog engage in shredding at the end of the treat hunt.

Need help remembering to save your toilet paper rolls? Place a cute little storage basket in your bathroom or by your recycling bin. This way, you'll have a visual reminder to keep them aside.

TIP

Paper Tube Snuffler

Food Motivation | Indoor | Shredding Outlet | Uses Recycled Items

Let your dog help you take care of those empty toilet paper tubes! They're perfect enrichment tools to bring into play for a variety of snuffle and shredding games. Don't have a big stock of tubes on hand just yet? Try cutting what you have in half, to double your supply in a pinch. Then spread the word that you're starting a collection to your friends and family who don't have dogs of their own.

WHAT YOU'LL NEED

- **Shallow box (think: short and long)**
- **Toilet paper tubes (I used 24)**
- **Dry treats of choice**

SCENT SCIENCE

- **Helps dogs collect important information on their environment**
- **Aids in decision-making**
- **Boosts learning**
- **Helps them recognize people and places**
- **Evokes pleasant feelings and even memories in our canine companions**

STEP BY STEP

1. Find an appropriately sized box for your pup. Don't make it too tall, or they won't be able to get to the treats.

2. Fill the box with toilet paper tubes so that they are standing up and touching.

3. Shake some dry treats over the box so that they fall into the tubes.

4. Serve to your pup.

The Powerhouse to the Brain

Think of your dog's nose as a powerhouse that continually feeds information to the brain. Out of all the senses, scent is one of the most important ways that our dogs interact with the world around them.

TIP

Always put away the fleece strips after the supervised game ends; don't leave them hanging around for curious mouths.

Snuffle Cinnamon Buns

Food Motivation | Good for All Ages | Indoor | Sensory Experience

Time for bun fun—no need to turn on the oven! This snuffle puzzle looks appetizing to your dog and pretty enough to post on your socials. A muffin tin and folded fabric bring the enrichment magic. It's easy to assemble as a fun way to get your dog discovering and learning through a food- and texture-based experience.

WHAT YOU'LL NEED

- **12 fleece strips (approximately 1½ inches wide x 22–24 inches long)**
- **Dry treats of choice**
- **6-cup muffin tin**

LOVE FOR FLEECE STRIPS

- **Simple to wash and reuse in other games**
- **Add extra challenge in an egg carton puzzle (page 43)**
- **Great texture element in a scentsory box (page 40)**
- **Perfect for the end of a flirt pole (page 89)**
- **Can add scents to strips as bonus stimulation**

STEP BY STEP

1. Lay six fleece strips on a flat surface. Set the remaining six strips aside until step 3.

2. Place a line of dry treats on each of the six strips.

3. For each strip topped with treats, take one of the reserved strips and place it on top of the treats, essentially sandwiching the treats between two layers of fleece.

Wiggle Those Vibrissae!

Touch is an integral way dogs interact with their environment. Besides using their paws to feel different textures and surfaces, dogs also experience touch with their bodies, mouths, and even through touch-sensitive hairs called vibrissae (whiskers) on their nose and chin and above their eyes. As they make their way through their Snuffle Cinnamon Buns, watch how your dog navigates touch between the different textures of the activity.

4. Roll each strip sandwich from bottom to top, creating a neat little way to capture the treats.

5. Place each roll on its side inside a cup of the muffin tin. The swirl should be facing up.

6. Serve to your pup.

Understand Foraging Fun

Here's an experiment to try with your dog that may just blow your mind.

- Prep a bowl of food and set it aside.
- Take the same type and amount of food and place it inside a puzzle of some sort—maybe a wrapped towel, an enrichment box, or an interactive feeder.
- Then place the two options in front of your dog. What option do they go for?

You might be surprised to find that your dog will often pick the puzzle. There's a term for that preference: *contrafreeloading*. It's the behavior seen in most animals when they choose food that requires effort over no-strings-attached food access. But why not take the free lunch?

When it comes to dogs specifically, it's important to recognize that they have deeply sown genetic tendencies when it comes to foraging. Instinctively, a dog's senses are tuned to look for food. So much so that the act of searching and foraging for food can be more of a thrill for your dog than the actual act of obtaining the food itself. This instinct that's itching to be fulfilled is why food puzzles, toys, and activities can be so enjoyable for dogs—even before they enjoy a taste of the reward.

One classic study with monkeys measured feel-good dopamine spikes in a work-for-food situation. The monkeys were given a light as a signal that they could press a button in front of them to receive food. Guess when dopamine levels in their brains skyrocketed? At the signal and during "the work" of pressing the button, not when receiving the food reward. It wasn't even close.

Researchers conclude that food excitement is greatest in the anticipation. Even when "free" food is readily available, food puzzles, snuffle mats, and stuffable toys are enjoyable to most animals—dogs, monkeys, and even raccoons and chickens.

Like most things in life, there are some exceptions. Studies find that animals must have a reliable food source available before contrafreeloading kicks in. (A starving animal will not care for puzzles.) Additionally, one species didn't follow the contrafreeloading trend: standard house cats. Probably not a surprise to many, house cats tend to prefer free meals.

One more important note is that while animals may like to work for their food, we mustn't make these activities too difficult. Always ensure you're modifying games and activities to set your dog up for success. You want activated pleasure centers in your dog's brain, not frustration.

TIP

Always use dry treats in these tubes, as any sort of damp treat will soak into the paper. This can be very enticing (but not healthy) for curious mouths to try and eat!

Treat Tumblers

Indoor | Quick Setup | Shredding Outlet | Uses Recycled Items

If you haven't started saving empty toilet paper tubes, today is Day One. They're DIY enrichment gold! Watch your dog's eyes light up while you laugh off the looks from family and friends when they all see a towering box full of toilet paper rolls that you're saving. Priceless.

WHAT YOU'LL NEED

- **Empty toilet paper rolls and/or paper towel rolls**
- **Dry treats of choice**

LOVE FOR PAPER TUBES

One of the reasons why paper rolls of all kinds work great for canine enrichment is because of their movement. They're small and skittery—something that dogs are extremely tuned in to because of their innate drive for prey.

STEP BY STEP

1. Twist and scrunch one end of a tube to close the opening.

2. Add dry treats through the open end of the tube.

3. Twist and scrunch the open end of the tube to close.

4. Repeat with additional tubes, if desired.

5. Serve to your pup.

Level It Up

Want to make your dog's tumblers more challenging? Try pairing them with a tissue box. Simply follow steps 1 to 4 above, then stuff the tubes into an empty tissue box. Your dog will love digging into the box to find their treat tumblers!

To make the puzzle a bit more difficult, only put treats in certain, not all, cups of the muffin tin.

TIP

Hide-and-Treat Tin

Emphasis on Choice | Food Motivation | Great for Puppies | Shredding Outlet

This muffin tin puzzle is a fun but accessible way to hide treats and offer a blend of sensory and foraging enrichment. It was one of the first DIY enrichment puzzles I ever made for Bindi. So simple to put together, it's perfect for puppies still learning and rising to the challenge.

WHAT YOU'LL NEED

- **Dry treats of choice**
- **12-cup muffin tin**
- **Crinkly brown paper (optional)**
- **Assortment of toys**

LOVE FOR MUFFIN TINS

- **They're great for hiding treats.**
- **Balls fit for easy cover.**
- **They come in handy for serving tastes of yogurt, peanut butter, or frozen treats.**
- **Dishwasher-safe tins make for easy cleaning.**

STEP BY STEP

1. Place dry treats in the cups of the muffin tin.

2. For crinkle and texture, add strips of the brown paper (if using) over every treat or just select treats.

3. Place toys on top of the treats in each muffin cup.

4. Serve and watch your dog use their nose to find their treats.

Easy Variety

Crinkly paper is a great addition to a DIY puzzle like this for many reasons. Not only is it easily accessible, but it also adds an element of sound (cue the crinkly, skittery sound that dogs love so much!) and fun shredding texture. You can swap in toilet paper rolls (discussed on page 51) or some snuffle cinnamon buns (on page 47). If you have a notorious gulper, try iceberg lettuce (yes, lettuce!) that we discuss on page 85.

Tasty Treats & Stuffers

Thinking outside the bowl is a great way to add novelty to your dog's routine. If your dog is food-motivated, they will love the sensory activation and anticipation of solving a food puzzle. For any dog, slowing down the feeding process is beneficial for digestion and adds a cognitive challenge to a familiar part of their day. Try these simple ideas and feel your bond grow as you treat your dog to healthy homemade fun! Ingredient amounts are based on a large stuffable toy, but feel free to adapt for a different size or your dog's needs.

Stuffing in Five Steps

Before we get to a ton of fun, ready-to-go recipes, and options for your dog, a few beginner tips can help the experience go smoothly for you and your furry friend. These helpful suggestions can also inspire you to create recipes of your own that your dog will love.

1. MAKE INTRODUCTIONS

KONG, meet dog. Dog, meet KONG. Well, not *exactly* like that. But a common mistake people make when giving their dog a new stuffable toy is not introducing it properly.

Sometimes, a dog will dive into a frozen, filled treat toy with no issues. In other cases, a dog may need guidance and encouragement to learn that they're able to get what's inside—and that what's inside is worth their time. Stuffable toys can be confusing and frustrating for a dog who has never encountered one, so taking it slow helps ensure that your dog has a good transition. For a successful start:

- **Keep size in mind.** While a stuffable size may look right at a glance, trust the sizing guides provided on enrichment toys. And never rush your pup, thinking they will grow into a size. When enrichment toys aren't engaging (or accidents happen), the cause is often size-related.

- **Set up an easy win.** Start with loose treats inside an empty KONG. This kind of stuffable is bouncy and rollable, just the enticement your dog needs. Your pooch will want to explore and soon realize that the new beehive toy has obtainable rewards inside.

2. LEVEL UP

If your dog gets the hang of the loose treats with no sweat, you can begin to gradually level up your stuffable game. Try wet stuffable goodies (like peanut butter, yogurt, and moist meats), then graduate to frozen stuffed toys.

At every step, watch your dog's body language and take note if something seems too difficult for them. You want to create enrichment, not frustration. So while a frozen treat may last long, it can also cause angst for certain dogs. More time doesn't always mean more enjoyment.

3. BROADEN THE MENU

Imagine you ate the same sandwich every single day. Although it might taste great the first day, even the first week, it would get old pretty quickly. One way to keep your pup engaged in edible enrichment is to add and rotate through dog-safe ingredients that keep things new and exciting. You'll find some great starter ideas in the Enrichment Grocery Shopping List on page 59. No more boring same-old sandwiches or stuffables!

To make safe, smooth food introductions:

- **Go slow.** Incorporate new foods one at a time. Give the ingredient to your dog in your

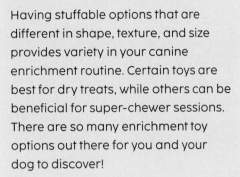

Toy Hunting Fun

Having stuffable options that are different in shape, texture, and size provides variety in your canine enrichment routine. Certain toys are best for dry treats, while others can be beneficial for super-chewer sessions. There are so many enrichment toy options out there for you and your dog to discover!

presence 24 to 48 hours before stuffing it into an enrichment toy. This allows you to monitor for any allergic or intolerant reactions.

- **Get expert advice.** Always touch base with your vet if you're unsure whether a certain food or add-in is good for your dog.

4. LAYER FOR INTEREST

While there's no exact science when it comes to enrichment stuffing, how you stuff enrichment toys can help keep your dog engaged enough to work through an entire treat. For this reason, I find that a layering method works great. You'll find examples of these layers throughout the recipes in this chapter.

Bottom: High Value

Pack a high-value treat inside the bottom of the enrichment toy. The high-value treat works to keep your dog interested in making their way through the entire treat.

Middle: Filler

The filler should be something for your dog to work through. I like using a mix of wet and dry ingredients, as I find that the different textures keep my dogs engaged.

Top: Taste Teaser

Choose something tasty to stick out of the top of an enrichment toy. Think about what might grab your pup's interest through their senses.

5. FEED IN BALANCE

Enrichment toys are an amazing way to add value to your dog's treats and meals, but we need to be careful not to go crazy with them to the point of overfeeding. To find a balance:

- **Keep daily needs in mind.** Touch base with your vet if you're unsure of how many calories per day you should be giving your dog. Although rough calorie calculators are available online, only your vet can base a goal on your dog's breed, age, activity level, health history, and other individual considerations. Knowing their needs will help you build treats into your dog's routine and make ingredient choices based on calorie count.

- **Break out a meal portion.** A great way to incorporate edible enrichment into your dog's feeding routine is by serving a portion of your dog's meals inside toys. It takes the guesswork out of calorie counting and adds more excitement at mealtime.

Enrichment Grocery Shopping List

Here are our go-to ingredients that you should be able to find at any standard local grocer. Nothing fancy required.

Proteins

- Chicken (cooked, shredded or ground breast)
- Eggs (chicken, quail, or duck; if utilizing shells, farm-fresh is best)
- Protein-packed treats (such as dehydrated beef liver or chicken heart treats)
- Salmon (freshly cooked or low-sodium canned variety/packed in water)
- Sardines (fresh at the meat counter or canned/packed in water)
- Turkey (cooked, shredded or ground breast)

Fruits & Veggies

- Apples (cored and seeded)
- Bananas
- Blueberries (go for fresh—frozen blueberries tend to make a big purple mess)
- Broccoli
- Carrots
- Celery
- Cucumbers
- Green beans
- Herbs such as parsley, basil, and mint
- Lettuce
- Mangoes (peeled and seed removed)
- Peaches (pit removed)
- Raspberries
- Strawberries
- Sweet potatoes (cooked)

Binders

Binders are wet ingredients that can hold all of your ingredients together inside the enrichment toy. Essentially, they're the "glue" for stuffing. Think teaspoons and tablespoons over handfuls and cupfuls when starting out.

- Applesauce (natural with no xylitol or added sugars)
- Baby food puree packets in flavors such as sweet potato, carrot, and green bean (choose organic and ensure dog-safe ingredients)
- Chicken or beef broth (low-sodium with no onion added)
- Cottage cheese (low-fat)
- Goat's milk
- Greek yogurt (plain, xylitol-free)
- Kefir
- Pure pumpkin puree (not to be confused with pumpkin pie filling)

Avoid using ingredients that are toxic to your pet, such as chocolate, onions, garlic, grapes, raisins, and anything with sweeteners or sugar substitutes (such as xylitol). Additionally, steer clear of ingredients that may cause choking or digestive issues, such as bones, rawhide, and large chunks of food.

TIP

Save "pup cups" from takeout treats to wash and reuse with DIY versions.

Pupkin Spice Cup

Food Motivation | Good for Sensitive Dogs | Good for You Too | Uses Recycled Items

This festive fall treat is a tempting sensory experience that's also super-healthy for your dog. Kefir is an excellent source of probiotics beneficial for gut health, while turmeric offers anti-inflammatory properties that promote joint health and reduce skin irritation. Feel free to make an extra cup—replacing the dog treat with a gingersnap or biscotti—and join in the enjoyment!

WHAT YOU'LL NEED

- **Small plastic cup**
- **¼ cup + 2 tablespoons pure pumpkin puree**
- **1 tablespoon plain kefir**
- **Pinch of turmeric**
- **Whipped cream**
- **Dog treat of choice**
- **Ground cinnamon**

LOVE FOR PUMPKIN

- **Rich in potassium for muscle health**
- **Supports eyes, skin, and coat with beta-carotene**
- **Provides vitamin C for stronger immunity**
- **Serves up fiber for healthy digestion and weight**
- **Reduces instances of both diarrhea and constipation**

STEP BY STEP

1. Fill the base of the cup with 2 tablespoons of the pure pumpkin puree.

2. In a small bowl, mix the remaining ¼ cup of pure pumpkin puree with the kefir and turmeric. (You can add more kefir to reach the desired lightness in color.) Add to the cup as the middle layer.

3. Top with a bit of whipped cream, the treat, and a sprinkle of cinnamon.

Make Your Own Puree

Preheat the oven to 350°F. Line a baking sheet with parchment paper. Cut a pumpkin in half or quarters. Scoop out the seeds; save them to roast later if you like. Place the pumpkin halves or quarters skin side up on the baking sheet and bake for about 2 hours. You'll know the pumpkin is done when the skin peels off easily. When cool enough to handle, remove all the skin. Mash the pumpkin with a fork or puree in a blender for a smoother texture.

Pupper-mint Stuffer

Food Motivation | Good for Sensitive Dogs | Indoor | Soothing

Gone are the days of peanut butter as the only stuffer choice. You can discover lots of fresh ways to provide tasty enrichment for your dog. Most dogs love a creamy treat of yogurt, and it loves them back with health benefits. Just keep it plain and simple—avoid yogurt with added sugars, artificial sweeteners, sugar substitutes, or toxic fruits. In this stuffer combo, cucumber adds low-cal, high-fiber crunch, and a little mint promotes better breath and digestion.

WHAT YOU'LL NEED

- **Stuffable toy (such as a KONG)**
- **½ cucumber, cut into half or quarter slices**
- **1–2 tablespoons shredded cooked chicken or kibble (optional)**
- **2 or 3 fresh mint leaves, stems removed**
- **¼ cup low-fat or nonfat plain Greek yogurt (ensure no xylitol on the ingredients list)**

LOVE FOR YOGURT

- **Packed with probiotics for gut health**
- **Provides protein for muscles and metabolism**
- **Supports strong teeth and bones with calcium**
- **Neutralizes bacteria that can cause tooth decay**

STEP BY STEP

1. In an empty egg carton or shot glass, place the stuffable toy with the opening facing up.

2. To begin creating the layers, press half of the cucumber slices into the bottom of the stuffer.

3. Add three-quarters of the chicken or kibble (if using) as the next layer.

4. Add one or two mint leaves.

5. Using a small spoon or squeeze bottle, fill the stuffer to about the three-quarter-full mark with the yogurt.

6. Add the remaining cucumber slices except for one piece followed by the remaining yogurt. Gently tap the stuffer on the countertop to allow the yogurt to settle into all the crevices.

> **TIP**
>
> Always save a portion of your stuffing ingredients as a garnish to immediately entice your pup.

THE HAPPIEST DOG ON THE BLOCK

7. Top with the reserved cucumber slice, remaining chicken or kibble (if using), and the remaining mint leaf.

8. Freeze the stuffer overnight, keeping it in the empty egg carton or shot glass and with the opening facing up.

9. When ready to treat your pup, remove the stuffer from the freezer.

Stay Away from Xylitol

Even small amounts of the sugar substitute are toxic for dogs. And it's popping up in more and more products in your grocery store—including some yogurts, nut butters, ice creams, and candies. Always read labels, and call your vet if you suspect ingestion of a dangerous ingredient.

@bindisbucketlist

Tail-Wagging Breakfast

Food Motivation | Indoor | Soothing

Dogs can look forward to an eggs-and-bacon breakfast as much as you do. In our household, this recipe is a special weekend treat for Bindi and Rosie while the humans enjoy some hot breakfast and downtime as well. It's the perfect start to everyone's day! Plan to prep ahead so you can freeze it overnight and make the treat last longer for your dog.

WHAT YOU'LL NEED

- **Stuffable toy (such as a KONG)**
- **2 dry treats of choice (optional)**
- **1 piece cooked bacon**
- **2 fresh parsley sprigs**
- **1 hard-boiled egg, shell removed and halved**
- **⅛ cup bone broth or water**

LOVE FOR EGGS

- **Great source of protein**
- **Provide omega-3 fatty acids to support healthy skin and coat**
- **Multiple ways to serve (hard-boiled, scrambled, even raw—I add a cracked egg right into my dogs' meals weekly)**

STEP BY STEP

1. In an empty egg carton or shot glass, place the stuffable toy with the opening facing up.

2. Add one dog treat (if using) to the bottom of the stuffer. Set the other aside to add to the top later.

3. Cut the bacon into small pieces and sprinkle into the bottom of the stuffer.

4. Add one sprig of the parsley.

5. Take a half of the hard-boiled egg and squeeze it into the opening.

6. Using a small spoon, squeeze bottle, or measuring cup, add the bone broth or water. (It may begin to run out the bottom, but that's okay. Just get the ingredients wet enough to stick together while in the freezer.)

7. Add the remaining dog treat and parsley so that they're sticking out of the top to entice your dog.

8. Freeze the stuffer overnight, keeping it in the empty egg carton or shot glass and with the opening facing up.

9. When ready to treat your pup, remove the stuffer from the freezer.

PB & Banana Smoothie Mat

Food Motivation | Good for All Ages | Indoor | Soothing

Smoothies are a special treat for dogs too! Try serving this classic flavor combination on a lick mat, which is simply a grooved mat that encourages the act of licking. Usually made of thermoplastic rubber (TPR) or silicone, most lick mats have individual patterns and textured surfaces that create a grazing maze. These textures and patterns help lock food in so that your dog actively licks at their meal or treat, as opposed to the normal chomping and gobbling.

WHAT YOU'LL NEED

- **Blender**
- **1 banana (fresh or frozen)**
- **3 tablespoons natural peanut butter**
- **½ cup plain kefir**
- **Pinch of ground cinnamon**
- **Lick mat**

LOVE FOR LICK MATS

- **Fulfill licking instinct in a healthy way**
- **Release endorphins (feel-good brain chemicals) as your dog licks**
- **Help your dog calm down in stressful situations**

STEP BY STEP

1. In the blender, combine the banana, peanut butter, kefir, and cinnamon. Pulse until smooth.

2. Place the lick mat on a tray that can be easily transferred to the freezer.

3. Pour the smoothie mixture onto the lick mat, using a spatula or spoon to smooth it over the ridges. Or use a squeeze bottle (try reusing a clean honey bottle) to make lick mat prep a breeze. Fill as desired.

4. Place the lick mat in the freezer for 2 to 5 hours.

5. Remove from the freezer and serve.

> **TIP**
> Any leftover smoothie mixture can be placed in a freezer-safe storage container and frozen for up to 3 months. Then just defrost as needed. Or pour the extra mixture into an ice cube tray for quick and easy pupsicles!

Licking Good Times

Some ingredients that are perfect to include on a lick mat are cottage cheese, gelatinous bone broth, natural peanut butter (xylitol-free), plain Greek yogurt, pure pumpkin puree, veggie purees (such as green bean and carrot), and wet dog food.

Beyond the ingredients, here are a few tips and tricks for lick mat success.

Have a mat flipper? Use a tray. Simply place the mat inside a baking tray or tin when feeding. This extra layer of protection helps discourage pups who are notorious for picking up their lick mats and trying to flip them over. Just as enjoyable with less mess!

Teach your dog proper use. Creating boundaries helps your dog stay safe and get the most out of their treat. It also keeps the mat in good condition for the next enrichment session. If your dog pulls at the mat, redirect this behavior so that they know how to use the lick mat the correct way. Put the mat away as soon as your dog is finished foraging to discourage any rough play. You can even say "All done" as a signal as you take it away. Setting up an end to the game helps keep it interesting too—your dog might get bored spending time with an empty lick mat.

Look out for your licker. The mat should only be used when you're around to watch your dog use it. Certain dogs, when finished, will flip the mat or try to tear at the sides. Make sure you're there to supervise and stop this behavior with redirection to proper use.

Make cleaning easier. All of those little maze crevices make great spots for extra food to lodge itself—a benefit when your dog is exploring but a bit of a pain when you're cleaning later. Your best bet: soak the mat in warm, soapy water immediately after your dog's use. Then go back with a scrubbing brush to dislodge anything left behind. Most lick mats are also dishwasher safe (top rack, leaned up against a plate).

TIP

Adding a small tray or cutting board under your mold helps to balance your ingredients while freezing.

Pupsicles

Food Motivation | Good for All Ages | Outdoor

Without a doubt, pupsicles are my favorite treat to make for my dogs in the summer. They're easy to whip up in batches, completely customizable, and help keep the dogs cool, comfortable, and entertained. Choose ingredients with health benefits to make ice pop treats work even harder for your pooch.

WHAT YOU'LL NEED

- **Fun ice pop mold**
- **Wet ingredient of choice (I used a portion of raw meal)**
- **1 bully stick, sized appropriately for your dog**
- **Kefir or plain Greek yogurt**

LOVE FOR BULLY STICKS

- **Easily digested by dog's stomach**
- **Single ingredient: beef muscle**
- **High in protein**
- **Source of amino acids, which support muscles, brain, skin, and coat**
- **Help maintain clean teeth**
- **Can be enjoyed by dogs of any breed, age, or size**

STEP BY STEP

1. Press the wet ingredient of choice into the base of the ice pop mold.

2. Place the bully stick so that it will be the ice pop's stick.

3. Flash freeze for 1 hour. This will make the bottom layer firm up a bit, stop the ingredients from mixing too much, and set the stick.

4. Remove the mold from the freezer.

5. Add the kefir or yogurt on top to fill the mold.

6. Freeze for a minimum of 4 hours. (The exact freeze time will depend on the size of your mold.)

7. When ready to serve, remove from the mold.

No Bully Stick? No Problem

Use ice cube trays instead of a mold to create fun frozen treats that can used in many ways—around the yard, popped into stuffable toys, or for Backyard Fishing (page 103).

Chicken Bone Broth

Food Motivation | Good for All Ages | Good for You Too

I get asked for this recipe *all the time*. And it's no wonder. Sure, you can get store-bought chicken broth, but many of the options in your grocery store are packed to the brim with salt, dog dangers (like onions), and other unwanted additives. Making your own broth ensures you know exactly what it contains. And the process is easier than you might expect! Plus, *you* can enjoy the delicious (healthy) results as well.

WHAT YOU'LL NEED

- **Multicooker (such as an Instant Pot)**
- **Raw chicken bones (such as wings, backs, necks, or feet*) or a whole raw chicken**
- **Water**
- **2–3 tablespoons apple cider vinegar**
- **1 or 2 large carrots, halved (optional)**
- **1 or 2 celery stalks, leaves on and quartered (optional)**
- **Fresh sprigs of parsley, rosemary, sage, and/or thyme (optional)**

* If you're looking for a thick, gelatinous bone broth, add more chicken feet and don't overdo it on the water. Chicken feet are rich in collagen—the key to a rich broth.

LOVE FOR BONE BROTH

- **Rich in collagen to support joints, skin, and coat**
- **Improves overall digestive health**
- **Offers health benefits for dogs and people**

STEP BY STEP

1. Insert the multicooker grate and place the chicken bones inside the pot. If you're using a whole chicken, place it inside on the trivet.

2. Fill the pot with water until it just covers the chicken bones.

3. Add the apple cider vinegar.

4. Allow the bones, water, and vinegar to sit for a few minutes while you chop the carrots and celery (if using). Don't be tempted to skip this step! The vinegar draws nutrients out of the raw bones, but the flavor of vinegar will not be present in the broth after cooking.

5. If using the vegetables, add them.

6. If using the herbs, add a few sprigs of your choice.

7. Seal the multicooker and cook on high for about 2 hours.

8. When the cooking time is complete, do a natural pressure release. Once the pot is depressurized and safe to open, remove any large bones with tongs and discard.

  Note: Do not feed any cooked bones to your dog. They are extremely dangerous.

9. Allow the broth to cool to room temperature.

10. Strain the remaining bones and solid ingredients as you transfer the contents of the pot into a large bowl. A fine colander lined with cheesecloth works well.

11. If using the broth immediately, skim any fat off the top and serve. If saving the broth for later use, chill for at least 6 hours. Broth can be stored in the fridge for up to 3 days or in the freezer for up to 3 months. Portion it first if you plan to freeze.

Cook It Your Way

While a multicooker makes this recipe much faster, you can also use a slow cooker or turn to your stovetop. For either of those methods, the broth will need to cook much longer. Bring the broth to a boil and then simmer on low for a minimum of 12 hours. Bone appétit!

Pup Pizza Party

Food Motivation | Good for All Ages | Good for You Too

Dogs and pizza are an amazing combo! When Bindi turned four, we celebrated her special day by treating her to a pupperoni pizza. The dog-friendly dough is made with plain Greek yogurt, a healthy addition that the humans in the household will enjoy as well.

WHAT YOU'LL NEED
Dough

- 1 cup nonfat plain Greek yogurt
- 1 cup whole wheat flour or all-purpose unbleached flour
- 1 teaspoon cornmeal, for dusting (if using a pizza peel and pizza oven)

Dog-Friendly Toppings of Choice

- Plain tomato sauce (no onion or garlic in ingredients)
- Shredded chicken
- Crumbled beef
- Sardines or anchovies (canned/packed in water)
- Pepperoni
- Pineapple
- Mozzarella cheese
- Broccoli
- Cooked carrots

LOVE FOR HOMEMADE PIZZA

- **Customizable ingredients**
- **Can be made low-sodium and low-fat**
- **Option to skip or go light with the cheese if your dog doesn't tolerate cheese well**
- **Most of all, so fun to share with your dog!**

STEP BY STEP

1. Mix the yogurt with the flour until the dough comes together. Using your hands, shape the dough into a soft ball.

   Note: This dough will be stickier than your average pizza dough.

2. Place your dough ball on a floured surface and roll it into a circle with a rolling pin. Optional: Press your fingers into the dough about 1 inch from the edge to create a more defined crust.

> **TIP**
>
> Don't want to give your dog tomato sauce or can't find a pup-friendly option? Try using cooked, mashed veggies for the first layer.

7. Return to the oven and bake until the toppings are cooked to your liking, about 5 to 10 minutes.

8. Let the pizza rest for about 5 minutes before slicing. Allow a portion to cool before serving to your dog.

To bake in a pizza oven:

3. Preheat the oven to 350°F. (Because of the density and wetness of this particular dough, it cooks better at a temperature lower than you might bake a traditional pizza dough.)

4. Add your toppings of choice.

5. Dust a pizza peel with cornmeal (to prevent sticking), then place the pizza on top to transfer to the oven.

6. Continuously turn the pizza to ensure even cooking, about 15 to 20 minutes (pizza ovens may vary).

7. Let the pizza rest for about 5 minutes before slicing. Allow a portion to cool before serving to your dog.

Follow the next set of steps based on your cooking method.

To bake in a standard oven:

3. Preheat the oven to 400°F. Cover a pizza (or general baking) pan with parchment paper.

4. Transfer just the rolled dough (with no toppings yet) onto the pan.

5. Bake the dough until the bottom is golden, about 15 minutes.

6. Remove the crust from the oven, then top your pizza as desired.

Canine Birthday Cake

Bond Building | Food Motivation | Good for All Ages | Indoor

What's a birthday without a cake? Tailor your cake to what your dog likes best! I've included the toppers and "icing" my dogs love. Other good options: applesauce (dog-safe variety), blueberries, goat's milk kefir, peach (no pit), pineapple (small amount), salmon oil, sardines, and shredded chicken.

WHAT YOU'LL NEED
Cake

- 1 tablespoon coconut oil
- 1½ cups all-purpose flour
- 1 teaspoon baking soda
- ½ teaspoon baking powder
- ½ teaspoon ground cinnamon (optional)
- ¼ teaspoon salt
- ¾ cup pumpkin puree
- 1 ripe banana
- ¼ cup chunky natural peanut butter
- 2 large eggs
- 1–2 tablespoons honey

"Icing"

- ½ cup pure pumpkin puree
- 3 tablespoons melted coconut oil

Cake Toppers

- 8 kiwi slices
- 3 or 4 raspberries
- 6 dog treats of choice

STEP BY STEP

1. Preheat the oven to 350°F. Grease two loaf pans with the coconut oil. Set aside.

2. In a medium bowl, whisk together the flour, baking soda, baking powder, cinnamon (if using), and salt. Set aside.

3. In a large bowl, with an electric mixer or by hand, beat the pumpkin puree, banana, peanut butter, eggs, and honey until well combined. Add the dry ingredients and mix just until combined.

4. Divide the batter evenly between the two prepared pans. Bake for 25 to 30 minutes, or until a toothpick inserted in the center comes out clean.

5. Cool in the pan for 10 minutes.

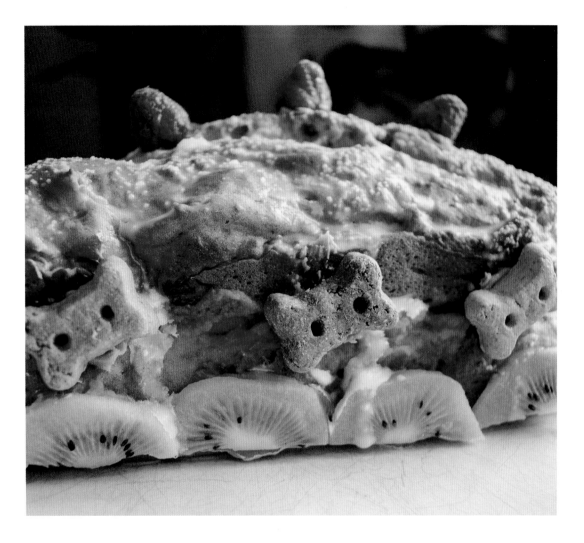

6. Invert the cakes onto a wire rack to cool completely.

7. Bind the layers together with most of the pumpkin puree "icing." Save a bit to attach the toppers.

8. Drizzle the melted coconut oil over the cake.

9. Top with cake toppers of choice, using the remaining pumpkin puree to hold.

Frozen Layered Cake

If baking isn't your forte, you can still treat your birthday dog to a special cake. For many birthdays, I've opted to make my dogs mini frozen cakes. Simply use a freezable plastic storage container to create the form. For extra fun, try using three different size containers to create stackable layers.

First, place plastic wrap or parchment paper into the bottom of your container(s). This step will help you pop out the frozen cake easier when the time comes. Then add your ingredients of choice and freeze for at least 4 hours.

DOG-FRIENDLY INGREDIENT IDEAS

- Wet dog food
- Plain kefir
- Blueberries
- Pumpkin puree
- Sardines
- Shredded or ground chicken breast
- Plain yogurt
- Bone broth

When you're ready to serve a single-layer cake, run the bottom of the frozen container under warm water for a minute. Then, pull on the wrap or parchment to help the layer pop right out. Decorate as desired, and let your pup enjoy!

To make a multilayered cake, run the bottom of each frozen container under warm water for a minute. Then pull on the wrap or parchment to help the layers pop out. Stack the layers as desired and run the entire cake under a cool tap for a split second—to help the layers stick together. Place the cake back in the freezer for about an hour. Decorate, then celebrate your dog!

TIP

For an extra treat, add a bit of bone broth (recipe on page 72) along with the kefir into each muffin cup.

Muffin Lick Tin

Food Motivation | Good for All Ages | Indoor | Soothing

A standard muffin tin is an easy and inexpensive tool to mirror the way lick mats and slow feeders lock food in place. Any kind of grooves, divots, and spaces slows down the gobbling and makes your dog think about their meals and treats. Incorporating these novel feeding techniques into your dog's routine is a great way to keep them interested and learning.

WHAT YOU'LL NEED

- **6-cup muffin tin**
- **Tray (optional)**
- **Plain kefir**
- **Dry treats of choice**

LOVE FOR KEFIR

- **Packed with protein and vitamins**
- **Offers bone-building calcium**
- **Good source of gut-healthy probiotics**
- **Cow's milk variety is low in lactose**
- **Also available produced from goat's milk, coconut milk, rice milk, and oat milk**

STEP BY STEP

1. Place a clean muffin tin on a tray (if using). Using a tray underneath the tin can make it easier to steady in the freezer.

2. Using a knife or spoon, spread the kefir into the tin's cups.

3. Place a treat in the center of each kefir portion.

4. Freeze until the ingredients are set, about 2 to 4 hours.

5. Remove and serve.

Keep It Simple

When feeding your dog kefir, choose unsweetened and unflavored varieties. It's perfect for lick mats and tins. You can also drizzle kefir over a meal, mix it into a recipe for a stuffable toy, or combine it with dog-safe fruit like blueberries or apples to freeze for pupsicles.

TIP

You may need to encourage your dog with your hands if they're a bit stumped. For example, tear some pieces of the lettuce off with your fingers.

Edible Shreddables

Indoor | Sensory Experience | Shredding Outlet

It's no surprise that dogs love to rip and shred. While most people try to deter the behavior completely, shredding is considered an innate canine behavior. It's not necessarily something that can be "trained out" of a dog. Instead, giving your dog proper outlets and guidance can help stop unwanted chewing, ripping, and shredding (your shoes or couch) while allowing them to find fulfillment in a safe and monitored way. Enter edible shreddables!

WHAT YOU'LL NEED

A dog-safe, shreddable veggie, such as the following:

- **Head of iceberg lettuce**
- **Broccoli stalks**
- **Celery**
- **Parsley**
- **Carrots**

STEP BY STEP

1. Wash your vegetable of choice.

2. Serve the veggie and watch how your dog chooses to interact.

Differences in Shredding

Not all shredding activities are created equal. Dogs shred for different reasons.

- **Healthy outlet:** We as owners provide a shredding activity, puzzle, or toy in a safe, monitored way with proper cues to alleviate our dog's innate need to shred.
- **Sign of boredom:** Your dog suddenly tears apart something they've come across in your home for no apparent reason.
- **Sign of anxiety:** Maybe your dog shreds a blanket when you leave the house or bites the drywall at the door entry where they see you leave for the day.
- **Sign of frustration:** If a puzzle or game is too difficult or your dog doesn't understand, it often leads to frustration. As a result, your dog leans toward what they instinctively know how to do: shred and chew.

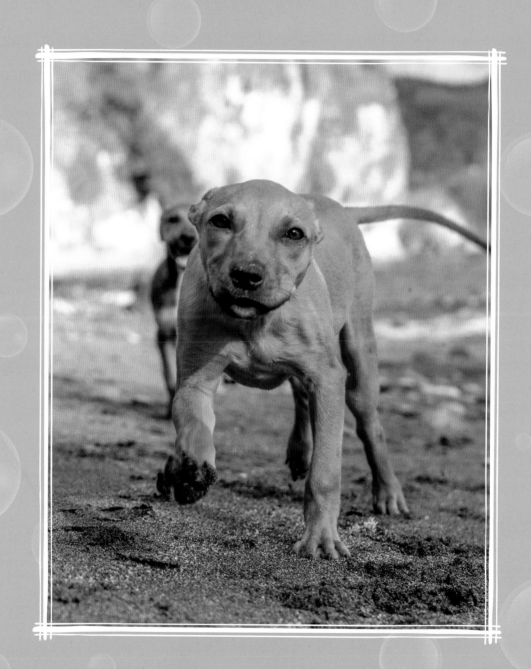

The Thrill of the Chase

This chapter is especially dedicated to the movers and the shakers! For many dogs, there's nothing quite as exciting as the *go, go, go* or even the *zoom, zoom, zoom*. Providing some level of physical outlet is good for all dogs, but the enrichment hits a new level when you can combine physical *and* mental exercise for your companion in the same activity. If you're looking for that happy-tired feeling for your friend, you've come to the right place.

Part of the fun of this chasing game is also the catching. You don't want your dog to get frustrated because they're never able to catch the lure.

TIP

Flirt Pole Play

Bond Building | Cognitive Challenge | Energy Outlet

Many dog owners think they don't know what a flirt pole is—until I mention the smaller forms used for cat play. It's essentially a pole with an attached lure that you make dart around. The movement of the lure activates your dog's prey drive and offers a healthy outlet for chasing. You can use lures with different textures, sounds (think crinkly), and even scents to intrigue your pup. But a flirt pole is all you need to create a chase game and burn lots of energy!

WHAT YOU'LL NEED

- **Flirt pole (that's all!)**

LOVE FOR FLIRT POLES

- **Relatively inexpensive to buy and very easy to DIY**
- **Great option for people who may have physical limitations (for example, cannot take their dogs on lengthy daily hikes to tire out their pups)**
- **Amazing tool for teaching impulse control and commands like "Wait," "Leave It," "Drop It," and "After It"**

STEP BY STEP

1. Find a space large enough for your dog to run around (such as an empty yard or a large indoor space without obstacles).

2. Begin by placing the lure on the ground and moving it in a quick, dragging movement. Avoid lifting the lure off the ground or encouraging jumping.

3. Allow your dog to chase the lure and be sure to allow them to catch the lure as well.

TIP

Choose treats that fit properly into your enrichment feeders. You want your dog to have success, not frustration.

Chomp & Chase

Energy Outlet | Food Motivation | Indoor | Quick Setup

Some feeders use sight, movement, and sound to encourage your dog to engage in brainwork. These moving enrichment toys will especially appeal to dogs who like to dig in their bowls and create prey games at mealtime. With the toys' help, you can introduce a fun, food-chasing outlet for any dog that doesn't require cleanup. As the enrichment toy moves around, your dog can get a little activity while hunting and tapping into the contrafreeloading instinct (page 47).

WHAT YOU'LL NEED

- **Loose, dry treats of appropriate size**
- **Enrichment feeder that requires movement, such as a KONG Wobbler, Bob-A-Lot, or Snoop**

STEP BY STEP

1. Place the treats into the enrichment feeder.

2. If it's your dog's first time interacting with the feeder, get down on your dog's level and show them how the activity works. Knock and move the enrichment toy to release food as your dog watches.

3. Offer encouragement and praise your dog when they get things right. This can make the game even more enjoyable for our furry friends.

4. When the treats are gone, always remove the toy. This will help show your dog that treats are gone = the game is over (and will also help your toy last longer).

Make Your Own Moving Feeder

Simply recycle an empty plastic coffee container. Using a drill, make treat-sized holes throughout the clean canister. The number of holes and their placement will affect how many treats come out and at what rate. When you want to give your dog feeding fun, place treats in the container and pop the lid on. Ready to roll!

TIP

My dogs and I love using tennis balls or the small ZippyPaws burrowing toys for this game.

Gopher Hole

Cognitive Challenge | Indoor | Nonfood enrichment | Uses Recycled Items

This game will take you back to retro arcade days and Whac-A-Mole while it fulfills some of your dog's most basic instincts. It uses sight and motion to encourage your dog to engage in acceptable prey play. Utilizing small toys and "peekaboo" movements, you'll create an active puzzle that your dog will love.

WHAT YOU'LL NEED

- **Small toy or ball**
- **Paper towel**
- **Shallow cardboard box (I used a shoebox)**

STEP BY STEP

1. Start by choosing the toy you're going to use as the "gopher." This step is important, as the size of the hideaway item will help you decide the size of your box and holes.

2. Set the gopher on a paper towel. Draw a circle that fits completely around the toy with a bit of margin space. Cut out the circle. This will be your guide to cut holes in the hiding box.

3. Using the guide, trace circles onto the box. (Using a shoebox and a tennis ball, I was able to fit six evenly spaced holes.)

4. Cut the circles out of the box.

5. Cut a small semicircle into the side of your box. This is access for your arm.

6. Place the box on the floor. Pop the toy up through a hole. Mimicking Whac-A-Mole movements, allow the toy to reappear and dart back into the box again.

7. Allow your dog the satisfaction of "catching" the toy.

Dissecting Diversion

Your gopher hole puzzle box (page 93) isn't just a one-trick game. You can use your cardboard creation to make a fun dissecting activity for your pup.

Simply fill the box with paper, balls, or small toys, then let your dog fish them out through the gopher holes. Rosie (pictured in her unicorn glory!) loves it when we use the ZippyPaws burrowing toys. They're the perfect small size for this game.

You may be scratching your head a bit as to why an activity centered around letting your dog dissect toys might fit in a chapter titled "The Thrill of the Chase." After all, the activity seems pretty sedate. The reason it fits perfectly links back to something called the *canine predatory sequence*. Dissecting, ripping, and shredding are all steps within this sequence.

There are roughly five stages within the canine predatory sequence. Knowing the stages can help us understand why our dogs love certain enrichment games so much. Our dogs' predatory sequence flows as follows:

1. The Search is the act of finding something to catch—whether it's actual prey, a tennis ball, or even a canine companion in a prey play game. This stage can utilize any and all of your dog's senses. They may follow a scent, follow a sound, or look for skittery motion.

2. The Stalk can bring an intense gaze as your dog analyzes their prey. They'll try to predict movement while stealthily inching closer.

3. The Chase is the pursuit, often at full speed. It's a great way to burn some physical energy—whether your dog is chasing prey, Frisbees, balls, or bubbles!

4. The Bite is sometimes also called The Catch/Kill. While it sounds ominous, it's an important part of the sequence that you will see played out even with toys. The catch often looks like a pounce and snatch, then comes giving the toy a good shake for the "kill bite."

5. The Dissect/Consume is the finish. Ever wonder why some dogs love to rip the fluff out of their toys or even their beds? It's their natural drive. That's why finding positive outlets through enrichment options is so important!

Some dogs will get a greater thrill than others from games that highlight the predatory sequence. Terriers, collies, and hounds in particular love this flow of play. But a wide variety of dogs enjoy parts of or variations of a predatory sequence. Think: stalking toys, chasing tennis balls, pulling tug toys, and even dissecting soft toys. When you realize the connection, it's quite easy to spot predatory sequence play!

Crinkle Ball

Indoor | Shredding Outlet | Uses Recycled Items

While this enrichment game uses a crinkle sound to intrigue your pooch, it also offers a fantastic shredding and dissecting outlet. (For more on dissecting behavior, see page 95.) Pairing brown paper with any stuffable ball will do the trick, but our household loves the versatile JW Hol-ee Roller. It can be played with as is or used in a variety of enrichment puzzles for your dog.

WHAT YOU'LL NEED

- **Paper bags**
- **Dry treats of choice (optional)**
- **Stuffable ball, such as the JW Hol-ee Roller**

THE SCIENCE OF CRINKLING SOUNDS

Whether from a bag of food opening or a paper bag pulled out for enrichment, the sound of crinkling can bring hounds running to investigate. Scientists believe that the love of crinkle sounds has a genetic link. Our dogs' brains are tuned to seek prey, and the crinkling reminds them of the sound of scurrying prey. No wonder it's an enjoyable experience for many dogs!

STEP BY STEP

1. Rip the paper bags into large strips.

2. Wrap the treats (if using) in the paper bag strips.

Rolling Success

To keep stuffable balls at just the right level of challenging fun for your dog:

Start easy. Allow your dog some time to get used to the activity and how it works.

Watch stuffing size. You can gradually increase the difficulty but never make it impossible. If you have a hard time getting something in or out of the ball with your thumbs, imagine how hard it will be for your dog using only their mouth!

Modify as needed. If you have a dog who fixates on paper, opt for towels. If you have a dog who is food-motivated, make sure to add treats.

If you have a mega chewer, you'll want to remove the ball as soon as the activity or game is complete.

TIP

3. Stuff the paper bag strips into the roller. Ensure that large pieces of crinkly paper stick out of the holes—this should look a little wild and wacky. You don't want the ball packed extremely tightly or it will make the strips very difficult for your dog to remove—and lead to frustration.

4. Throw the crinkle ball low across the ground. Then watch as your dog begins their chase, followed by shredding and dissecting (and chomping any treats).

As you're adding the sand or dirt, you can also bury some dog toys for your dog to find.

TIP

Dig Pit (Temporary)

Digging Outlet | Nonfood enrichment | Outdoor | Sensory Experience

Dogs have an instinct to dig that is deeply rooted in their genetic heritage. However, this activity is often seen as a nuisance or "naughty" behavior because it tends to affect your beautiful garden beds. By providing a designated digging space for your dog, you can encourage this natural behavior in a positive way while also protecting your landscaping. If you're unsure whether your dog would use and enjoy a dig pit, you can set up something temporary to give your dog a dry run.

WHAT YOU'LL NEED

- **Plastic kiddie pool (or a children's sandbox)**
- **Play sand or loose dirt**
- **Cover (this could be a wooden cover or a tarp)**

LOVE FOR A TEMPORARY DIG PIT

- **Can be used on a trial basis**
- **Works well if you don't have a place where you can commit to a permanent dig pit (such as rental properties)**
- **For places with a variety of seasons, can be used for outdoor digging in the summer, then be emptied for indoor enrichment games in the winter**

STEP BY STEP

1. Find a prime place in your yard for the kiddie pool. Keep in mind that the pool will be extremely heavy once filled, so it's easier to set up your place in the yard before adding the sand. You also want to avoid a need to relocate once it's filled.

2. Add the play sand or loose dirt to the kiddie pool.

3. Introduce your dog to the pit and redirect all digging behavior to the pit. Be sure to praise and reward your dog when they dig in the pit. This redirection and positive reinforcement combo will help your dog associate their digging behavior with their digging pit. In time, they will go straight to the digging pit on their own.

4. Always cover the dig pit at the end of a play session. Protection will discourage bugs, critters, and yard debris and keep the pit dry and ready for digging.

Dig Pit (Permanent)

Digging Outlet | Nonfood enrichment | Outdoor | Sensory Experience

If you know your dog is dig-obsessed and want to construct something more permanent in your yard, there are a variety of ways to do so without breaking the bank. Here are some options for what you can use to construct a permanent dig pit for your pooch.

WHAT YOU'LL NEED

- **Outside area where you can allocate space**
- **Play sand or loose dirt**
- **Border material (such as wooden two-by-fours or bricks)**
- **Cover (such as a wooden cover or tarp)**

LOVE FOR A PERMANENT DIG PIT

- **It may hold up better for longer than a kiddie pool or sandbox.**
- **It works well if you have space to commit.**
- **Your dog will be trained in one digging place; you won't need to watch where you position it each season.**

STEP BY STEP

1. Map out where you'd like to have the permanent dig pit in your yard. It's important to place the pit in an area with good drainage that's away from common areas. This will inhibit dirt or debris flying over your patio, or rainwater collecting somewhere into a makeshift bog.

The Dirt on Digging Behavior

Dogs dig for many reasons, including:

Enjoyment. Digging is a great way to relieve boredom. The digging motion can be exhilarating for dogs, and different textures like sand and soil can provide a novel and stimulating experience.

Hiding high-value items. Some dogs bury their favorite toys and treats to hide them from others. It provides a sense of safety and comfort.

Seeking prey. Dogs with high prey drive may dig after rodents and small animals.

TIP

Rake the dig pit regularly to sift out debris and keep the sand or dirt from hardening over time (which happens with exposure to certain elements).

2. Once you've mapped out a location, it's time to start digging. How wide and deep you dig is your preference, but dig at least a few inches into the ground. (If you don't commit, your dog may not either!) When you've reached the desired pit size, fill the pit with play sand or loose dirt.

3. Surround the border of the dig pit with wood or bricks. This will help keep the sand or dirt enclosed in the pit while also giving a good visual identifier of where the yard ends and the dig pit starts.

4. Introduce your dog to the pit, and redirect all digging behavior to the pit. Be sure to praise and reward your dog when they dig in the pit. This redirection and positive reinforcement combo will help your dog associate their digging behavior with their digging pit. In time, they will go straight to the digging pit on their own.

5. Always cover the dig pit at the end of a play session. Protection will discourage bugs, critters, and yard debris and keep the pit dry and ready for digging.

Backyard Fishing

Outdoor | Sensory Experience | Water Play

You don't need to wait for beach travel to treat your pup to a splash of fun! Pool play is a great way to offer enrichment to water-loving pups, especially on hot summer days. A game of backyard fishing with toys or simply ice cubes offers sense stimulation, prey-instinct satisfaction, and a way to stay cool and hydrated.

WHAT YOU'LL NEED

- **Kiddie pool**
- **Floating "prey," such as ice cubes, pupsiscle cubes (page 71), balls, and/or toys**

LOVE FOR POOL PLAY

- **Gives dogs who love water the sensory experience they crave right at home**
- **Offers cool relief and hydration on hot days**
- **Can even be used (gently!) for bath-nervous dogs to help them make positive associations with water and lower grooming stress**

STEP BY STEP

1. Place the kiddie pool in a location that will make it easy to fill and drain and is safe for your dog. Add water.

2. Add the ice cubes, pupiscles, and/or floating balls and toys to the kiddie pool.

3. Introduce positive play in the water with your pup. Move the cubes around, toss a few extra in the pool (midgame), and encourage your dog to grab their treats. Never force your dog into the water. When making introductions to water play (or any game!), give your dog the choice to participate and go slowly so as not to cause fear in a new situation.

Check the Temp

Water play requires appropriate weather and water conditions. You want the touch of the cool water to feel nice, not shocking, on their skin and coat. Try slightly warmer water if your dog seems averse to cool-water touch.

Some brands offer dog bubbles that appeal to pups with featured scents, including rotisserie chicken, bacon, and even cheese!

Bubble Mania

Energy Outlet | Indoor and Outdoor | Quick Setup | Works Well for Multiple Dogs

There's just something about bubbles that brings joy! They're so simple yet they provide an exciting energy outlet for children and dogs alike. When it comes to dogs, bubble bursts are an easy chasing enrichment that can work indoors or outdoors. They're fun little floating prey that can encourage your dog to be active and agile while also offering mental stimulation.

WHAT YOU'LL NEED

- **Child-safe bubbles**
- **Bubble blower or multi-bubble wand (optional)**

LOVE FOR BUBBLES

- **Initiate active play, even jumping**
- **Work agility and coordination**
- **Offer a chance to track prey**
- **Provide novelty to stimulate your dog's mind**
- **Can bring stress relief for you as a result of the type of breathing used to blow bubbles**

STEP BY STEP

1. Find the right space for bubble activity. This should be an open area free of obstacles, where your dog has proper footing.

2. Place bubbles in a bubble blower, or blow a few bubbles with a bubble wand.

3. Show your dog what to do, as needed, to introduce the activity.

Space to Launch

Excited dogs love to *zoom*! That's why having proper footing is always important when introducing games that initiate chasing or running. You want your dog to have space to launch, not injury risk after takeoff.

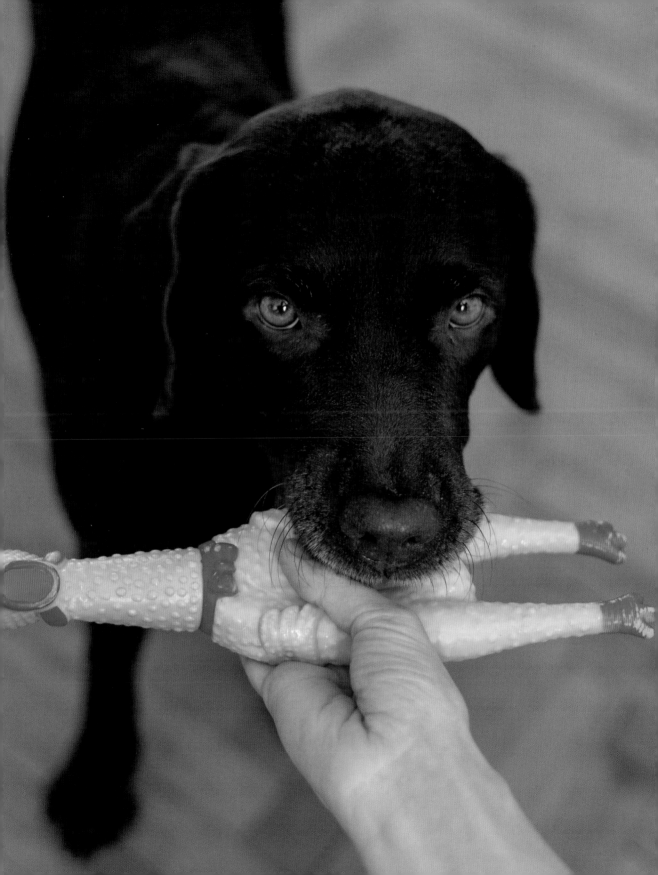

Squeak & Seek

Bond Building | Cognitive Challenge | Indoor or Outdoor | Quick Setup

An easy and fun take on traditional hide-and-seek, this game encourages your dog to use their senses and troubleshooting skills to find you at home. Keep it super simple if your dog is prone to separation anxiety; you want a nervous dog to have success.

WHAT YOU'LL NEED

- **Squeaky toy**

LOVE FOR SEEKING GAMES

- **Activate your dog's senses**
- **Boost your dog's problem-solving skills**
- **Reinforce their listening and recall skills**
- **Teach them not to panic if you're not in view**

STEP BY STEP

1. Armed with a squeaky toy, pick a hiding place away from your dog.

2. Squeak the toy at different intervals. If your dog is having a hard time orienting with just the squeak, feel free to call their name as well, at first.

3. Allow your dog to follow their ears, engage their nose, and use their senses to find you.

4. Celebrate your dog's win and reward them when they arrive at your hiding place.

> **TIP**
>
> Start with simple indoor hiding places first, so that you can slowly build up your dog's confidence. This could be somewhere like behind a couch or under a table. It's okay if your dog sees you during the first few rounds.

Herding Ball Play

Cognitive Challenge | Energy Outlet | Outdoor

A herding ball offers a unique form of enrichment for dogs who love this "job." If you have a herder, you'll see the behavior come out as they try to direct other pets in the household and even you! They may even gather objects such as socks. But you can give them an outlet with herding balls, which are larger and heavier than other balls you can buy. They are designed to stay on the ground and move in a way that your dog can steer—pushed and chased, as opposed to thrown and bounced.

WHAT YOU'LL NEED

- **Herding ball (such as a Jolly Egg or CollieBall)**
- **Treats of choice**
- **Clicker**

LOVE FOR HERDING PLAY

- **Helps dogs focus and work out energy**
- **Exercises natural instincts in a positive way**
- **May prevent nipping other pets and family members**
- **Especially good for herding breeds such as Australian shepherds, border collies, and German shepherds**

STEP BY STEP
Desensitizing the Ball

1. Introduce the ball to your pup. This is best done in a large, safe space such as a field or gated grassy area. The more space, the better—herding balls work best where your dog has space to run.

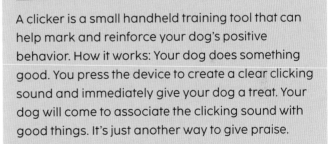

Make It Click

A clicker is a small handheld training tool that can help mark and reinforce your dog's positive behavior. How it works: Your dog does something good. You press the device to create a clear clicking sound and immediately give your dog a treat. Your dog will come to associate the clicking sound with good things. It's just another way to give praise.

2. Let them become familiar with their ball. It might take some getting used to because of the large size. Use positive reinforcement (treats and/or a clicker) and praise whenever your dog interacts with the ball. Interaction includes even little steps like sniffing and nudging.

3. Once a positive association is built, continue to reward your dog whenever they interact with the ball.

Teaching "Touch" & Movement

1. Follow the steps on page 119 to teach your dog the "Touch" command.

2. Once your dog has mastered the "Touch" command, cue your dog to touch their herding ball. Wait to mark and reward until the ball moves forward from their touch. Be patient and always offer encouragement; this may take lots of repetitions.

3. In time, your dog should be able to touch and move their herding ball on command. When this happens, begin rolling the ball in small stints to get them started, rewarding them for following the ball and using their nose to control the movement.

Build in Cues

Once your dog is comfortable with their herding ball and shows that they enjoy pushing it around, you can create more complexity through the use of different elements. Add obstacles to create more problem-solving opportunities or more herding balls to create a sense of choice. You can even go the extra mile to teach actual herding cues like "To Me," "Away to Me," and "Come Bye." For training tips and videos, search online for "herding cues."

Canine Connections

By now, it's probably clear to you that enrichment can bring lots of physical and mental perks to our dogs' lives. But maybe one of the most overlooked yet beautiful benefits is the way enrichment can strengthen the bonds between dogs and humans. With any kind of enrichment activity, your dog may show you appreciation after their enjoyment. Certain enrichment activities take that a step further, allowing you to enjoy the experience together in a special way. Don't worry, you won't need to carry anything in your mouth or dig in the dirt (unless you find it therapeutic)!

High Five

Bond Building | Cognitive Challenge | Good for All Ages

Teaching tricks not only keeps your pet engaged but also builds a stronger relationship between you and your dog. It can even help you understand your dog's learning style and improve your training skills while bridging the gap of understanding between you and your companion. In this enrichment training exercise, you will use visual cues to teach your dog a new trick.

WHAT YOU'LL NEED

- **High-value treats (my dogs' favorites are cut-up hot dogs and rotisserie chicken)**
- **Clicker (optional; for more on clickers, see page 109)**

LOVE FOR HAND CUES

Dogs cannot understand human language, but they can learn and communicate with us through different cues. Interestingly, a study on commands for canines revealed that dogs respond better to hand signals than voice commands. In the study, dogs responded to hand signals with 99 percent accuracy, compared to 82 percent accuracy for voice commands.

STEP BY STEP

1. Sitting on the floor, hold a high-value treat in your hand. Place your dog in a sit.

2. Make a fist around the treat and allow your dog to investigate your closed hand. Your hand should be at about shoulder height while seated on the floor with your knuckles facing the ceiling. Position your hand between you and your dog, not too close but not so far that they'd need to strain their arm to touch your fist. They may lick and try to open your fist but do not reveal the treat yet. Allow your dog to get to the stage of pawing your hand.

3. As soon as your dog paws at your hand, open your hand, let them get the treat, and mark this behavior with "yes!" Or if using a clicker, click to mark.

4. Repeat this sequence a few times. Always allow breaks if you find that your dog is not understanding or getting frustrated.

5. Once your dog has figured out the basics, you can begin to change your hand position. Lift your fist so that your knuckles are facing the ceiling and your palm is directly facing your dog. Keep repeating this sequence, rewarding the wins, until your dog's paw hits your palm each and every time. As your dog begins to understand this pattern, change your marker from "yes" to "High Five."

6. Next, advance to hold your open palm in front of your dog and say, "High Five." As soon as their paw meets your palm (as practiced), reward them.

7. Practice, practice, practice! Repetition will help your dog master the trick.

Take It to a Wave

The fun thing about this trick is that once taught, it can be easily transitioned into a super-cute "Wave" trick as well. Simply raise your hand as you would for "High Five" but a little farther away from your dog, so that their paw can't hit your hand right away. Using a clicker, mark when their paw is in the air (before it hits your hand). With proper positive reinforcement, your dog will soon associate your "High Five" hand as a cue to lift theirs as well, mimicking an adorable wave!

Touch Targeting

Bond Building | Cognitive Challenge | Good for Sensitive Dogs

The goal of "Touch," also called nose targeting, is to have your dog touch a target (first, your hand) with the tip of their nose. Where the nose goes, the head and body follow, making "Touch" an extremely handy little cue. You can use the cue in many different obedience or trick-training scenarios, but it can also be used in everyday life. Not only will it get you and your dog learning together, but it can also offer a sense of connection when the "Touch" cue is given and completed.

WHAT YOU'LL NEED

- **Sticky note**
- **High-value treats**
- **Clicker (optional)**

LOVE FOR THE "TOUCH" CUE

- **Gives your dog something to refocus on anytime you need it**
- **Can be used as a reassuring check-in between handler and dog**
- **Redirects nervous dogs in scenarios where they may be uncomfortable**
- **Provides a comforting alternative to anxious barking**

STEP BY STEP

1. Place a sticky note in the palm of your flat hand.

2. Invite your dog to investigate. Then give your dog a treat anytime they touch the sticky note with their nose. If using a clicker, also mark the action with a click.

3. Repeat, repeat, repeat. Once your dog enthusiastically associates touching the sticky note with rewards, mark this behavior as "Touch."

4. When your dog has nailed the "Touch" command, you can begin to create more distance between your palm and the dog. Continue to mark and reward your dog as soon as their nose reaches the sticky note.

5. In time, you should be able to remove the sticky note and use the "Touch" command only.

Introduce a "Drop" Command

You can use the fun and excitement of tug to teach a release cue. Begin playing tug with your dog, then gently ease up and end the resistance. Wait until your dog tires of pulling on their toy (they will soon get bored without the resistance) and drops it on their own. Praise them and reward them with another play session. Repeat this a few times until your dog associates the lack of resistance with dropping the toy. Mark the desired behavior with a cue word— "Drop," "Drop It," and "Release" are common cues.

Tug of Play

Bond Building | Energy Outlet | Good for Puppies | Indoor or Outdoor

You know this classic game as tug-of-war, but let's emphasize the interactive *play*. When it comes to tug, your dog's toy preference makes a difference. Do they prefer the sturdy grip of a rope toy or the bite of a firm silicone tug? A softer toy or something like a durable tug ball? When making your choice, keep your dog in mind. It'll make the play session that much more enjoyable.

WHAT YOU'LL NEED

- **Quality tug toy**
- **Willing participant**

LOVE FOR TUG GAMES

- **Satisfy predatory instincts**
- **Depend on another participant, resulting in collaboration and socialization play**
- **Strengthen muscles and coordination**
- **Offer a great opportunity to train commands, such as "Release"**
- **Can help build trust and confidence**

STEP BY STEP

1. Choose an open and safe space to play. Watch for a floor surface that offers your dog a sturdy sense of balance.

2. With your hands low to the ground, move the tug toy from side to side, not up and down. A good rule of thumb is to keep the toy in line with your dog's spine. You don't want your dog's neck stretched upward.

3. Tug to match your dog's enthusiasm, and try not to let go. This keeps the action fun and safe for your dog—suddenly releasing the toy when your dog is putting their all into the tug session can cause potential injuries.

4. Allow your dog to "win" during your sessions so they stay interested and not frustrated.

TTouch Ear Slides

Bond Building | Good for Sensitive Dogs | Soothing

For both pet owners looking to improve their animal's well-being and professionals working in animal care, the TTouch method offers a safe, effective, and gentle approach to animal care that can help to promote relaxation, well-being, and happiness. Created by Linda Tellington-Jones, the method centers around applying a variety of gentle touches, strokes, and circular movements to specific parts of an animal's body, such as the ears, paws, and tail. Ear slides are an easy starting place.

WHAT YOU'LL NEED

- **Your hands**
- **Willing dog**

LOVE FOR TTOUCH

- **Reduces stress and anxiety**
- **Strengthens human-animal bonds**
- **Nurtures body awareness, physical balance, coordination, and flexibility**
- **Especially helpful for animals who are nervous or anxious**
- **Can be used to support training and behavior modification**
- **Alleviates car sickness**

STEP BY STEP
Single-Hand Stroking

1. Starting at the lower base of one of your dog's ears (on the side of the head), gently stroke the ear with the fingertips of your index finger and thumb in the direction the ear grows. You will be moving from base to tip. Repeat on the other side.

OR

Two-Hand Stroking

1. Starting at each upper base of your dog's ears (on the top of the head), gently stroke each ear with the fingertips of your index finger and thumb in the direction the ear grows. You will be moving from base to tip.

> **Don't repeatedly stroke the same point over and over again; find new pathways with your fingers.**
>
> TIP

Complete the Sequence

2. With one hand, gently move the skin on the top of your dog's head in a clockwise circular motion.

3. Hold the base of one ear and move it in small gentle circles, clockwise first and then reverse to counterclockwise. Repeat with the other ear.

More Than Skin-Deep

The benefits of the TTouch method are not limited to physical relaxation. By helping animals to relax and focus, the TTouch method can also improve their ability to learn new commands and behaviors. It's an excellent training tool.

Goal Getters

Bond Building | Energy Outlet | Indoor or Outdoor

When we as humans work toward a specific, measurable goal, we're likely to feel increased confidence, a sense of purpose, a boosted mood, and more motivation. How about adding your dog to the equation? A furry companion can amp up accountability and the fun factor. Plus, you'll work on your confidence and compatibility as a team and experience all the emotional support that your canine cheerleader will bring.

WHAT YOU'LL NEED

- **Creativity!**
- **Planner or calendar app**

SAMPLE GOALS

- **Go on ___ walks a week.**
- **Go to one new place a week.**
- **Take on one new dog sport this year.**
- **Learn one new trick a week.**
- **Have a playdate with friends at least twice a month.**
- **Work toward maintaining a healthy weight.**
- **Collect ___ neat rocks together this year.**
- **Collect ___ sticks for a stick library.**
- **Try a new enrichment game every week.**
- **Ditch the bowl for fun enrichment feeders three times a week.**

Can Dogs Really Have Goals?

Dogs can hold short-term goals (think: catch that squirrel or grab that hot dog) but do not technically have long-term goal-setting abilities. That's where you come in! Long-term goals are something that we as pet parents can help set and achieve with our dogs. The SPIDER Framework is used by animal professionals around the globe to help create enrichment programs. While this framework can get incredibly in-depth, thinking about the bare bones of the framework can help us understand the benefits in terms of enrichment and finding what works best for our dogs:

S — **Set goals**
P — **Plan**
I — **Implement**
D — **Document**
E — **Evaluate**
R — **Readjust**

STEP BY STEP

1. Start by setting a goal for you and your pooch. (If you need inspiration, check out the ideas at left.)

2. Put your goal on your calendar app or in your planner, then keep track of your progress. The act of marking off or "completing" your goal (or steps toward your goal) for the week will help you stay focused and see your "wins."

3. Reassess at regular intervals. If your goal needs a bit of tailoring, no sweat! These goals aren't meant to make you feel stressed or under pressure. Rather, they are meant to be fun and to help you and your dog enjoy time together.

Bathing Beauty

Bond Building | Food Motivation | Indoor | Soothing

Enrichment has powerful outcomes. Some of the most rewarding to witness are when we can use enrichment to mitigate fear, anxiety, and stress (often referred to in the dog world as FAS). Helping your dogs in stressful situations is a surefire way to strengthen your bond while also helping them with positive ways to work through their feelings. One great place to use enrichment techniques to mitigate FAS: the dreaded bath!

WHAT YOU'LL NEED

- **Grippy bath mat**
- **Prepared lick mat with a suction cup or durable duct tape**

LOVE FOR MITIGATING FAS WITH ENRICHMENT

- **Helps dogs through scenarios that might be scary and stressful for them**
- **Serves as a comforting distraction**
- **Provides a positive association with the activity**
- **Decompresses dogs and releases pleasurable endorphins through use of a lick mat**

STEP BY STEP

1. Secure the bath mat in the tub to ensure proper footing for your dog.

2. If using a lick mat with a suction cup, stick it to the side of the tub or shower surface at the head height of your dog. If your lick mat doesn't have a suction cup, attach two giant duct tape loops (sticky side out) on the back of your lick mat and place it at the head height of your dog. Your dog shouldn't need to crane their neck to reach their treat.

How to Spot FAS

FAS stands for "fear, anxiety, and stress," which are all rooted responses to stressful scenarios and environments. A dog experiencing an FAS response may show physiological and behavioral changes, from mild signs of anxious body language (high arousal, stiff posture, firm gaze) all the way up to severe signs of fear (flight, freeze, fret, even aggression).

TIP

This calming enrichment technique can also be adapted to use with nail trims. Just set up on a rug instead of in the bathtub.

3. Bring your dog into the tub. Allow them to interact with their treat before starting the bath.

4. Start the water and slowly begin bathing your dog as they remain focused on their treat. Offer lots of praise and encouragement as you complete the bathing process.

5. Put the lick mat away as soon as the bath is complete. Your dog will come to associate the tub with the special treat.

These comfort tools can work in many situations that could be stressful for dogs—including having outdoor work completed around your home and hosting houseguests. Use enrichment activities as a tool for your dog's personal fear factors.

TIP

Firework Calm

Bond Building | Indoor | Soothing

There is a long-standing debate about whether offering your dog comfort during stressful situations is rewarding this behavior, in turn making it worse in the future. In my personal experience, this has never been the case. Fear is a visceral, powerful emotion that alerts our dogs (and us) to danger in order to keep them safe. If you know that your dog is afraid of fireworks, you can provide comfort and strengthen your connection with enrichment activities.

WHAT YOU'LL NEED

- **Stuffable toys**
- **Treats of choice**
- **Cozy resting place for your dog**
- **Calm white noise**

WHITE NOISE SOURCES

- **White noise machine or app**
- **TV on something calming (like a nature show or light music channel)**
- **Gentle playlist (search "sleepy dog" or "soothing dog" on apps like Spotify)**
- **Fan**

STEP BY STEP

1. Prepare some stuffed enrichment toys with your dog's favorite treats the night before the anticipated fireworks. Freeze the toys to make them last longer.

2. On the day of the fireworks, prepare a space where your dog can retreat—wherever your dog feels most comfortable and secure.

3. Begin playing white noise at dusk to help muffle the beginning of any fireworks.

4. As soon as the fireworks begin, serve your dog their frozen stuffed toy(s).

Doggy Day Out

Bond Building | Energy Outlet | Outdoor | Sensory Experience

The excitement of going places and interacting with their elements has many enriching benefits (for both canine and human alike!). Think about taking your dog to the beach. They get to feel the sand between their toes, hear the sound of birds overhead, see the water splash as they wade in, and smell salt, seaweed, and even nearby eateries. Maybe they get to dig a hole or swim or watch passersby. While the beach is a special place for Bindi and Rosie, any positive setting can work for your doggy's day out. Take the inspiration and modify as needed.

WHAT YOU'LL NEED

- **Long line or sturdy Flexi leash**
- **Comfortable harness**
- **Water**
- **Dog towel**
- **Treats**
- **Floating ball or fetch toy**

LOCATION, LOCATION

When it comes to picking your ideal Doggy Day Out location, individual preference and comfort are key. For some dogs, the hustle and bustle of an inner-city dog-friendly brewery might be a bit nightmarish, while an isolated hike on a new trail might be ideal. Some dogs may lean toward a meetup with some of their puppy friends, while others may prefer a solo dog visit to Grandma's house. Keep your dog's needs in mind.

STEP BY STEP

1. Do some research and pick your place. Especially for nervous and/or fearful dogs, this step is crucial to ensure that your dog is brought into a space that's paired well with their demeanor. For example, if you have a nervous dog, opt to hit the beach on a weekday or hit one of the less-crowded spots.

2. Attach the long line to your dog's harness, then let your dog enjoy a little exploration.

3. Assess your dog's body language and go with the flow. Is your dog enjoying themselves? Are they nervous? Are they thirsty? Do they need a break? Feel free to offer your dog some water and lay the towel down to give them a cozy spot to rest. Whatever their feelings may be, it's important to stay in tune with how they're taking in the new space. If they're scared, frustrated, or overwhelmed, what can be done to mitigate this?

4. Offer encouragement and treats as needed. In this space, you want your dog to just be a dog! Let them dig, run, chase, swim, sunbathe. Toss your fetch toy and enjoy the simple pleasures of the moment.

Bring high-value treats on outings. They're the best way to reward good behaviors and also create positive associations with certain places and experiences.

Errand Exploration

Bond Building | Outdoor | Sensory Experience | Socialization

A great place where most dogs are welcome in our area is our local greenhouse. Not only is this a great way to get you both out of the house and into the world, but it offers your dog some novel sniffing and socialization enrichment as well. As you run errands, take note of which local businesses are dog-friendly spaces and consider where your dog might be comfortable tagging along.

WHAT YOU'LL NEED

- **4- to 6-foot standard leash**
- **Comfortable harness**
- **Water**
- **Treats (preferably high-value)**

LOVE FOR DOG-FRIENDLY BUSINESSES

Our dogs bring many benefits to our mental and physical health as humans. One of these is a stronger sense of community. You can make connections through the dog-welcoming businesses and events in your area. These circles are generally filled with people who love and understand the everyday trials and tribulations of pet ownership, as well as the absolute joys. They "get" and support you and your dog.

STEP BY STEP

1. Do some research and pick your place. Especially for nervous and/or fearful dogs, this step is crucial to ensure that your dog is brought into a space that's paired well with their demeanor. For example, if you have a nervous dog, opt to try the greenhouse on a weekday or hit one of the less-crowded spots.

2. Attach your leash to the harness, then let your dog experience the greenhouse with you by their side.

3. Assess your dog's body language and go with the flow. Is your dog enjoying themselves? Are they nervous? Whatever their feelings may be, it's important to stay in tune with how they're taking in the new space. If they're scared, frustrated, or overwhelmed, what can be done to mitigate this? If they're thirsty, provide water. If they need a break, step out of the greenhouse to take a breather.

4. Offer encouragement. In this space, you want your dog to experience the novelty of the location in a confident yet calm way. Don't skimp on treats! Reward positive behaviors (such as calmly sniffing or checking in with you) to reinforce them.

The Wide World of Socialization

Many people think of canine socialization as dog-to-dog interactions only. But socializing your dog is a much wider umbrella! Socialization is preparing your dog for the world through interactions with places, people, environments, *and* other animals. It's helping your dog gain experiences and in turn learn how to cope with different people, places, and things. While the best time to socialize is in puppyhood, it's never too late to socialize.

Rolling with a Reactive Dog

Taking your dog out on the town provides great socialization and bonding time. But what happens if you have a reactive dog? You don't need to turn into complete hermits. You just need to feel confident and in control when you head out and roll with a reactive dog. These are the four steps I take with my dogs to ensure that we are as prepared as possible in a new environment.

Know Canine Body Language

Learning how your dog communicates with the world is an invaluable skill. By understanding and observing these behaviors in action, you'll find it easier to anticipate future stressors. As a result, it also becomes easier to intervene early and help your dog through difficult situations. Does your dog's tail go down? Ears go back? Hackles come out? Vocalizations that signal wariness? These are common nervous or fearful reactions, but you know your dog best. Watch for the earliest signs of anxiety in your dog.

Develop Situational Awareness

Stay alert to what's going on around you and how happenings (especially sudden changes) might affect your dog. While we don't necessarily want our dogs "living in a bubble," filtering our dogs' experiences can be key when mitigating FAS (fear, anxiety, and stress). Some situations are simply beyond their ability to comprehend and handle—this is where we can step in as guardians.

Identify Common Stressors

Every dog is an individual, and as a result, they'll have individual triggers and stressors. While it's not realistic to think that we can take away *all* of our dog's stress and discomfort, knowing what situations have an impact on our dogs helps us implement coping or avoidance strategies for their well-being.

Put Advocacy into Practice

Once you have a grasp on your dog's individual needs, you can then begin to put advocacy into practice. This can play out in different ways. Examples:

- You opt to leave your dog at home instead of taking them into an overwhelming environment.
- You step in and say no when someone approaches your dog to pet them.

Advocating for your dog will look different for everyone, but each scenario involving advocacy will strengthen your relationship and trust with your dog.

Pup Playdate

Energy Outlet | Outdoor | Socialization | Works Well for Multiple Dogs

Many dogs enjoy the company of canine friends. Some dogs find that social fulfillment at the dog park or doggy day care. For others, a quieter one-on-one meeting in a calm setting is a better experience. That's when a playdate is a perfect enrichment option!

WHAT YOU'LL NEED

- **Space with room to run and play**
- **Toy(s) of choice (optional)**
- **Treats**
- **Water**

THE POWER OF A PLAN

When setting up your playdates:

P — Plan with play styles in mind. Pairing dogs with similar demeanors can set everybody up for success.

L — Learn body language cues. Knowing positive and negative body language cues (especially in multi-dog scenarios) is incredibly important. Not only can it give you peace of mind, but it can also help you break up play when needed.

A — Always be present. Especially when dogs are new to each other, being present is vital to ensure positive introductions.

N — Never force interaction. Even when dogs are familiar with one another, never force an interaction. Always allow your dogs to have a sense of agency and choice in whether or not they want to participate.

STEP BY STEP

1. Have a meet and greet. Before letting the dogs play together, try taking your dogs on a group walk. This can allow your dogs to get acquainted in a calm, controlled setting.

2. Choose your space. The best place is a large, fenced-in area with room to run. For first interactions, consider a neutral space—some dogs can be particular about having new dogs in their space and yard.

3. Encourage positive interactions. Offering help and rewarding good behavior (with praise and treats) is never a bad thing.

4. Choose appropriate toys, or none at all. Some dogs can be extremely toy-obsessed and resort to resource guarding. If that's the case for either dog, leave out the toys. There is still lots of fun to be had!

Not All Dogs Love All Dogs

Playdates are only enriching if your dog likes socializing with other dogs. Look at the dog in front of you and celebrate the things they truly enjoy! If a pup playdate isn't an option, try bringing your dog to see one of their favorite people (a close friend or family member) for some loving. As long as you provide your dog with both mental and physical exercise and alternative social interactions (interactions with you, trusted friends, and select animals that your dog tolerates), your dog can live a very happy life.

5. Assess your dog's individual needs. If you find that they're looking thirsty, make sure that you provide an accessible source of water.

6. Assess the play. Are the dogs enjoying themselves? Are they a good match for play? Once you know that it's a good pairing, you can schedule your next outing.

From Appreciation to Zooeyia

Hopefully, this chapter has inspired lots of ways to nurture your bond with your dog—through shared enrichment games and adventures, supporting them in new or challenging situations, and even helping them expand their social circle. In return, you'll feel your dog's appreciation and love. And you'll also get *zooeyia* (zoo-AY-uh). No treatment required. In fact, it's good for your health! Zooeyia is a scientific concept that sums up in one word the benefits that interactions with animals have on human health.

While many of us know how happy our pets make us when we see them, you may be surprised to learn some of the ways that our animals positively affect our lives. Sure, they help us get exercise when we take them for a walk. They encourage us to play and not take ourselves too seriously. And they stimulate serotonin through their snuggles. But zooeyia dives into deep layers like communal impact and complex emotional impacts to see how our relationships with our animals influence physical, mental, and social well-being and even lifespan.

Documented individual benefits of interaction with animals include increased physical activity, smoking cessation, hypertension control, reduced anxiety, and treatment of post-traumatic stress disorder. Interaction with domestic animals contributes at the community level as well by facilitating social interaction, promoting a sense of safety, enhancing the "give and take" communication between neighbors and fellow pet owners, and perhaps even lowering overall health care costs.

It doesn't end there. Studies have shown that people with pets tend to have a higher rate of empathy than those without, as well as a stronger sense of community. Pet owners are 57 percent more likely to be civically engaged than non-pet owners. The benefits of companion animals have a halo effect, spreading through the community. So zooeyia is (thankfully) contagious.

Environmental Enrichment

Just like us, dogs gets stressed. And just like us, the right environment can have a calming effect. So while your dog may not enjoy lavender candles and weighted blankets like humans do, certain elements help them feel comfortable and confident at home. To be a truly enriching space, your dog's environment should provide choice, exploration, play, and opportunities for rest and relaxation. Don't worry, you won't need a home makeover to make this happen! Little (inexpensive) steps can help you add enriching elements that you and your dog will both enjoy.

Sniffy Wall

Good for You Too | Outdoor | Sensory Experience | Soothing

Dog-safe herbs and flowers can make any outdoor space exciting for their ever-busy noses and at the same time calming for their mood. Scent enrichment has been shown to lower stress in dogs. Not only are dog-safe plants a wonderful way to give your dog lots of scent variations, but plants can also add unique touch, taste, and sight elements into their daily lives. Plus, you'll get the calming benefits of green scenery and enjoy herbs you can use in the kitchen.

WHAT YOU'LL NEED

- Terra-cotta or plastic pots (4- to 8-inch size works well)
- Pot-holding brackets
- Space to secure them (We used two-by-four-by-eight wood pieces and two-by-four fence rail brackets to secure them to our fencing)
- Dog-friendly plants (see ideas below)

TIP

If your plant space gets full sun, terra-cotta might not be the best option—the pots will dry up very quickly.

DOG-FRIENDLY PLANT OPTIONS

- **Basil**
- **Campanula**
- **Columbines**
- **Dill**
- **Ferns**
- **Irish/Scotch moss**
- **Lavender**
- **Lilacs**
- **Marigolds**
- **Mint**
- **Parsley**
- **Rosemary (not recommended for dogs with seizure disorders)**
- **Snapdragons**
- **Thyme**
- **Violas (pansies)**

STEP BY STEP

1. Map out where you'd like to hang your pots. We measured our fence and added extra two-by-four panels equally spaced and secured by the fence rail brackets. This way, any screws we used wouldn't poke out the other side of the fence.

2. Screw in the pot holders at your desired spacing.

3. Fill the pots with fresh soil and transplant the flowers and herbs.

4. Place the pots in the pot brackets.

Pass By These Plants

It's always important to be mindful of plants that have toxic effects for our canine counterparts. When building a sniffy wall or garden, these are some plants to avoid: autumn crocus, azalea, daffodils, English ivy, lilies, lily of the valley, and tulips.

TIP

Do a little research to see what types of feeders attract different kinds of birds. Add as many feeders as you'd like.

Window Watching

Good for All Ages | Indoor | Sensory Experience

Ever see a little head at the window as you return home? Many dogs tend to "window-watch" as they wait for their pet parents. You can help your buddy feel more fulfilled while you're away with enrichment centered on observing the world in front of them. While you may think that something as small as adding a bird feeder outside might not make a difference, the fascination of watching critters is deeply ingrained within your dog. It's like Garden TV.

WHAT YOU'LL NEED

- **Bird feeder**
- **Birdseed**
- **Window that your dog frequents**
- **Comfortable perch**

STEP BY STEP

1. Fill the bird feeder with birdseed and place it outside. Make sure that the bird feeder is in the view from where your dog usually window-watches.

2. Encourage your dog's window watching by setting up a comfortable perch by the window.

In Tune with Nature

Dogs are hardwired with predatory behaviors that stem from their relation to wolves. While dogs may lack the full spectrum of color and detail resolution of their human counterparts, a dog's eyes are exceptionally responsive to movement, making critter watching exciting for them.

TIP

Hesitant hound? Feel free to sprinkle dry treats across the pathway. Using high-value treats can give nervous dogs the motivation to explore.

Sensory Pathway

Cognitive Challenge | Good for Puppies | Indoor or Outdoor | Sensory Experience

Dogs are naturally curious creatures who love to explore. So why not help your dog positively exercise that inquisitiveness by providing them with a multi-textured enrichment experience? Step by step, you can challenge your dog's senses and encourage them to think about where they're putting their feet.

WHAT YOU'LL NEED

- **Variety of different textures for your dog to step on/experience, such as bark/logs, concrete pavers, grass, mulch, pea gravel, sand, tires, shallow container of water**
- **Outdoor space clear of obstacles to set up the pathway**

LOVE FOR SENSORY PATHWAYS

- **Develop dog's cognitive skills as they analyze, observe, and investigate their environment**
- **Provide them with a fun way to exercise**
- **Stimulate their senses**
- **Excellent for bonding and creating memorable experiences together**

STEP BY STEP

1. Gather your materials and prepare the space where you'd like to set them up.

2. Arrange the materials to create a path of varying textures that your dog can explore. You can spread the materials in a circular pattern, in a straight line, or in any other pattern that you like.

3. Allow your dog access to their new sensory pathway. As your dog explores the environment, they will encounter different textures that they can feel on their paws. For example, sand will provide a soft and grainy texture, while pebbles will be harder and more uneven. They can dip their paws in the water.

Bring It Inside

Bad weather or no space outdoors? You can create a sensory pathway right in your living room with items of varying textures, such as pillows, wooden cutting boards, tiles, silicone baking mats, and small rugs.

Sensory Yard

Want to go bigger in your yard with sensory experiences? You have lots of options. When we moved into our first home in 2021, my husband and I knew we wanted to renovate our yard into a sensory paradise for Bindi and Rosie. (It's now a pretty sweet, relaxing space for us as well!) Our yard isn't huge, so we planned to make the most of every square inch. Here's inspiration for bringing sensory elements that will appeal to your dog (and you won't find shabby either) into your yard space.

PLANNING BY THE SENSES

Not sure where to start? Watch your dog and let them lead you to ideas. Use the checklist on page 151 to jot down ways you see your pooch using their senses to explore, have fun, and decompress. Then think about ways you could incorporate the experiences into your yard. The ideas that follow should help, but always feel free to modify for your dog and your unique situation.

Smell

Dogs "see" and interact with the world around them pretty intensely through their noses. Each little sniff may look ordinary, but with each twitch of the nose, your dog is decoding their environment. According to studies, a dog's sense of smell is a whopping ten thousand to one hundred thousand times stronger than that of a human!

Many studies on scent (or olfactory) enrichment with dogs show that it can help reduce stress-related behaviors and increase exploration.

Some possible sources of scent enrichment in a sensory yard:

- Dog-safe flowers, such as columbines, lilacs, marigolds, snapdragons, and sunflowers
- Dog-safe herbs, such as basil, dill, mint, and parsley
- Wet areas, such as ponds and swimming pools
- Dry areas, such as dirt, sand, and grass
- Birds/wildlife, welcomed by feeders

Sight

Incorporating different sights into a sensory yard can be as simple or as intricate as you'd

like. Whether you plant a wide variety of plant life, hang a bird feeder, or even add a small windmill or yard decorations of choice, the possibilities are endless. New sensory experiences can add variety to your dog's routine and make your yard a more interesting place to hang out.

Some possible sources of sight enrichment in a sensory yard:

- Diverse dog-safe plants and foliage
- Bird (including hummingbird) feeders, to bring in the sight of wildlife
- Wind spinners (be cautious in choices for nervous dogs)
- Yard decorations
- Play equipment

Sound

Auditory enrichment is perhaps one of the most overlooked categories when it comes to canine enrichment, and it shouldn't be. In fact, the ASPCA has an entire section on sound/auditory enrichment on its website. That's because sound can bring benefits for health and behavior by promoting relaxation and relieving boredom in dogs.

Some possible sources of auditory enrichment in a sensory yard:

- Water features (more on this on page 159)
- Plants that rustle in the breeze, such as Boston ferns and tall grass
- Gentle wind chimes
- Music speakers (classic rock, classical, and reggae are canine favorites, according to research)
- Again, bird feeders!

Touch

Think about the sensation you get when your feet touch grass for the first time after a long winter, or when your feet hit warm sand, or even when your hands grip a smooth rock. These are all very different sensations, and you can probably picture them in your mind's eye right away. Touch is a very important sense for dogs too!

Besides touch through their paws, dogs also experience touch with their bodies, mouths, and even through touch-sensitive hairs called vibrissae (whiskers) on their nose, chin, and above their eyes.

Some possible sources of touch enrichment in a sensory yard:

- Cool sand in a dig pit
- Running tunnels and/or raised standing areas
- River rock

- Water features
- Mulch (for dogs who don't consider it a delicacy!)
- Grass
- Long (dog-safe) ornamental grass, to run through or chew
- Dirt
- Pavers and/or patio stones

Taste

Taste is less refined in a dog than advertisements for food and treats may have you believe. According to the American Kennel Club, dogs have about seventeen hundred taste buds, whereas humans have

SENSORY YARD: FIVE SENSES PLANNER

List some things you may have observed your dogs using their five senses on to brainstorm!

SIGHT

SMELL

TOUCH

TASTE

SOUND

roughly nine thousand. But taste is still an important way that our furry friends explore the world.

Dogs can distinguish the same four taste categories as humans: sweet, sour, salty, and bitter. In addition, dogs have special taste buds geared specifically toward water that humans don't have. This genetic trait is believed to give dogs a stronger desire to drink water so that our dogs drink enough to maintain a healthy body function. A dog's sense of scent is also closely entwined with taste.

Some possible sources of taste enrichment in a sensory yard:

• Dog-safe flowers (you can choose flowers such as marigolds that are edible for humans too)

• Dog-safe herbs, such as basil, dill, mint, and parsley

- Dog-safe fruits and vegetables (cucumbers, green beans, and strawberries are favorites that work in a yard)

PLANNING FOR YOUR DOG

Now that you have an idea of the many possible elements you can bring into a sensory yard, let's talk about implementing the most suitable ones for your pup. The best part of creating a sensory yard is tailoring it to your individual dog's needs. Here are some examples.

Have a hound who loves to sniff?

Try adding natural snuffle mats by planting dog-safe grasses and florals. Two fun options: tufted hair grass and red switch grass. Do some research to find what fits in your space and climate. Aim for perennials so they'll come back each spring.

Have a dog who loves to dig?

Try providing your dog with their own personal dig pit (more guidance on pages 99–101).

Have an older dog who loves to lounge?

Try creating low, easy-to-access lounge spaces with soft grass, moss, or a comfy outdoor bed in a shady spot. Surround their favorite spot with some dog-friendly herbs and plants so that they can enjoy fresh scents in their space.

- Have a dog who loves water and gets hot easily?

   Try adding a kiddie pool, or if you've got the space, a dog-friendly pond! Not only can a water feature be super fun for dogs who enjoy water, but it can be a great cool-down spot on superhot days. Always monitor the water play.

Have a rambunctious puppy who loves to run and explore?

Try introducing some fun play elements to your sensory yard that involve climbing and exploration. Look at doggy day care setups for ideas. Anything from children's slides and play tunnels to entry-level agility features can work.

The most popular programming with dogs: virtual walks and nature shows (particularly with squirrels or birds). But believe it or not, Bindi also loves watching . . . the morning news! Find your dog's quirks and embrace them.

Canine TV

Indoor | Quick Setup | Sensory Experience

As Canadians, we definitely have days when we want to go outside with the dogs but the weather does not agree with us. We may play some relatively active indoor games, but the time comes when we need some additional easy enrichment options that don't require much monitoring. Some creative TV options can help.

WHAT YOU'LL NEED

- **TV or screen**
- **Access to YouTube (optional)**

TV TRUTH VERSUS MYTH

While a dog's vision is not as acute as their other senses, dogs can see TV and some of its colors (see page 177 for more on the black-and-white vision myth). Not all dogs are interested in TV, but some go crazy over certain programs.

STEP BY STEP

1. Before you set your dog up with some TV time, it's always good to check whether or not your dog truly enjoys it. (For example, in our home, Bindi loves TV while Rosie seems to be a bit on the fence about it.) To test, simply play some "virtual walks" on YouTube and/or some nature shows for your dog. Gauge your dog's interest in the content being shown.

2. If your dog responds positively to the TV test, you can now dive deeper into which type of content they enjoy watching the most.

3. Play your dog's preferred programming when you're busy at home and when you need to step out.

Programming Gone to the Dogs

Did you know that there is a premium cable TV/streaming network created specifically for dogs to watch? Created in 2012, DOGTV features programs for relaxation, stimulation, and even exposure training (lots of doorbells!). The channel caters to a dog's vision (more frames per second), hearing, and on-screen interests. But do they have morning news for Bindi?

Homebody Beats

Good for Sensitive Dogs | Indoor | Sensory Experience | Soothing

Canine enrichment is often associated with physical activities, such as playing fetch or going for walks, or food-motivated toys and games. But it's important to remember that dogs have more than just physical needs. Consider auditory enrichment. A study found that shelter dogs became more relaxed when exposed to music with a tempo of 50 to 60 beats per minute (bpm). You can turn on this type of music when you leave your pet alone at home or when you want to encourage them to have some quiet time.

WHAT YOU'LL NEED

- **Speaker**
- **Streaming service playlist (aim for 50–60 bpm)**

SONGS AT 50–60 BPM

- **"Fly Me to the Moon,"** Frank Sinatra
- **"Landslide,"** Fleetwood Mac
- **"Northern Wind,"** City and Colour
- **"Riptide,"** Vance Joy
- **"The Weight,"** The Band
- **"Trouble,"** Ray LaMontagne

STEP BY STEP

1. Create a puppy playlist of songs that are 50 to 60 bpm. If you want to use an existing playlist, you can search "50–60 bpm" on a streaming service like Spotify and find options that others have made.

Make Music a Choice

Research shows consistent benefits of playing music for canines—from physical effects on health to influence on behavior. That's not difficult to understand considering how much music can affect our human moods. But one study included an interesting but important point from researchers: to make auditory enrichment most effective, we should always offer our dogs autonomy over their musical environment. So simply have music playing in one portion of the house and peace and quiet in another, then let the dog choose their environment. Choice is a key part of enrichment.

2. Start by playing your puppy playlists when you're home and with your dog. This will get your dog accustomed to the music, and you can see if your dog prefers one type of music over another.

3. Once your dog is used to the music, you can start playing your playlists when you leave your house for work or to run errands. This way, your playlists aren't associated directly with you leaving (which could make the music anxiety-inducing to some dogs).

> **TIP**
>
> Always try to mix up your playlists. Studies have found that playlists with a variety of genres are the best for our dogs and that playing the same playlist over and over loses its enriching power over time.

Sunshine Sounds

Good for You Too | Outdoor | Sensory Experience | Soothing

Canines have a keen sense of hearing, and there are many ways that we can incorporate sound into their daily routines. Introducing new sounds, such as recordings of wildlife or city noises, can provide mental stimulation and keep your dog engaged. Playing music or white noise in the background can provide a calming effect for dogs and help them relax. You can even introduce natural white noise in your yard or on your balcony.

WHAT YOU'LL NEED

- **Large bowl, bucket, or flowerpot (with no drainage holes)**
- **Water**
- **Solar fountain**
- **Sunshine!**

MORE MAGICAL SOUNDS

To add additional sounds of serenity, consider:

- **Plants that rustle in the breeze, like Boston ferns**
- **Long ornamental dog-safe grasses**
- **Gentle wind chimes**

STEP BY STEP

1. Place your container somewhere in direct sunshine.

2. Add water to the container.

3. Place the solar fountain into the water.

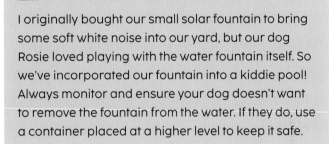

Monitor and Modify

I originally bought our small solar fountain to bring some soft white noise into our yard, but our dog Rosie loved playing with the water fountain itself. So we've incorporated our fountain into a kiddie pool! Always monitor and ensure your dog doesn't want to remove the fountain from the water. If they do, use a container placed at a higher level to keep it safe.

Suite Choices

Emphasis on Choice | Indoor | Nonfood enrichment | Soothing

You might be reading this one scratching your head, thinking, *Taylor, you've really lost it. Providing beds is . . .* enriching? To this, I would answer, *Yes, it is!* Having multiple comfortable places at home for your dog to choose for sleep may seem simple, but these little adjustments in our homes can have great benefits. It's all about agency—more on that on the next page!

WHAT YOU'LL NEED

- **2 or 3 dog beds, pillows, or blankets**

THE POWER OF AGENCY

- **Your dog's ability to have some kind of control of their decisions, environment, and life**
- **A way that dogs can learn from their choices**
- **Confidence builder**
- **An important piece of the enrichment puzzle**

STEP BY STEP

1. Start by looking around your home and identifying some of your dog's favorite spots. Consider the spaces your dog naturally gravitates toward—maybe in front of a sunny window, beside your bed, or by a heating vent.

2. Place a bed or create a comfy space with pillows and blankets in at least two new areas around your home.

3. Show your dog the newly furnished comfort zones, providing encouragement and praise to try them out.

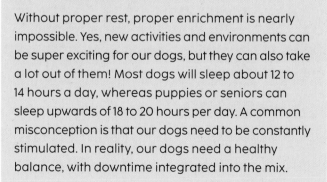

Everything in Balance

Without proper rest, proper enrichment is nearly impossible. Yes, new activities and environments can be super exciting for our dogs, but they can also take a lot out of them! Most dogs will sleep about 12 to 14 hours a day, whereas puppies or seniors can sleep upwards of 18 to 20 hours per day. A common misconception is that our dogs need to be constantly stimulated. In reality, our dogs need a healthy balance, with downtime integrated into the mix.

Not All Choices Are Equal

Giving your dog a choice between wanting to sleep in bed A or bed B, letting your dog choose the walking path while on a sniffari (page 35), and letting your dog choose which toys to play with during a play session are examples of healthy ways to provide a sense of agency. It's important to recognize that not all choices provide agency. For example, forcing your scared dog to choose between getting a treat from stranger A or stranger B does not provide agency; it's a coerced choice. Also, keep in mind that safety will always come before agency. Many dogs (if given the chance) would love to roam off leash, but due to safety concerns and leash laws, this is not a choice we can give our dogs freely and often.

TIP

For nervous dogs, the sound of a plastic kiddie pool can be overwhelming at first. To soften any stress, lay a towel or two at the base of the ball pit to muffle harsh sounds. That step will also add better footing for dogs who may not like the plastic base.

Pooch Ball Pit

Outdoor | Sensory Experience | Works Well for Multiple Dogs

Ball pits were so fun when we were kids. They can be just as entertaining for our canine companions! You can use them in a variety of ways to create easy, at-home sensory experiences completely tailored to your individual dog—from basic balls and water play to nature element exploration.

WHAT YOU'LL NEED

- **1 plastic kiddie pool**
- **Ball pit balls**
- **Treats (optional)**

LOVE FOR KIDDIE POOLS

- **They can be used in many different ways throughout the year.**
- **In the summer, fill with water for outdoor water play.**
- **In the fall, fill with leaves, pinecones, and sticks for sensory exploration.**
- **In the winter, bring inside and fill with towels and blankets for an XXL snuffle experience.**

STEP BY STEP

1. Place your kiddie pool in a location where it won't slide.

2. Add in the ball pit balls.

3. Encourage your dog to explore the ball pit. Sprinkle in some treats (if using).

Dogs Just Want to Have Fun

While it's very important to have elements in your home that allow your dog comfort (such as warm, comfortable beds), it's also important to have options that allow safe play. Whether it's a ball pit, a bucket of toys (page 165), a dig pit out back (pages 99–101), or a wide variety of feeder toys (page 91), having access to these outlets leads to a happier, healthier dog.

TIP

Make sure the height of your toy container is accessible for your dog. Aim for enrichment, not frustration.

Toy Bin Bonanza

Emphasis on Choice | Indoor | Nonfood Enrichment | Sensory Experience

If you're anything like me, you're sometimes left scratching your head when thinking about how many dog toys have made their way into your home over the years. Let's put those toys to work by encouraging your dog to use their facial whiskers (called vibrissae) to touch and go through a variety of different textures and materials.

WHAT YOU'LL NEED

- **Variety of dog toys of different textures and shapes**
- **2 large laundry baskets, boxes, or toy bins**

LOVE FOR TOY VARIETY

- **Having a number of accessible toys gives dogs a sense of choice.**
- **Swapping the selection of toys every one to two weeks keeps toys novel and exciting.**

STEP BY STEP

1. Collect all of the dog toys in your home. (You may need to do this stealthily when your dog is napping.) Divide the collection in half, aiming for a variety of textures and shapes in each grouping. Place in two separate toy containers.

2. Place one toy container out in the open, in an accessible space your dog can reach. Store the other toy bin where your dog won't find it.

3. Allow your dog to pick their toys from the in-use container throughout the week, engaging in play when they bring you something.

4. At the end of the week, swap out some toys from your stored-away bin. This will create a sense of novelty and give toys a higher value.

Make Old Toys New

Researchers published an interesting study in *Animal Cognition* that investigated how novelty plays a key role in our dog's toy choices. In this study, researchers presented three toys: two that the dogs were familiar with and then one that they had never seen before. Out of the fifty tests done, the new toy was chosen a whopping *thirty-eight* times! The study shows us the importance of keeping things new and exciting for our dogs, and how dogs can grow tired of the same old toys when used again and again.

However, this finding doesn't mean that we need to be shelling out wads of cash every week to keep our dogs entertained. Instead, here are some ways you can keep old toys exciting and novel:

- **Rotate your toys,** as discussed in Toy Bin Bonanza (page 165).
- **Pair toys with new enrichment games.** For example, use tennis balls in DIY puzzles or stuffed toys in enrichment boxes.
- **Add scent to give toys new life.** You can roll a toy in grass or leaves, treat with dog-safe herbs, or use a dog-designed commercial scent spray.
- **Play together.** Oftentimes, dogs are left to their own devices when it comes to play. Playing together can make toys increase in value to our pets. If your dog doesn't resource guard, you can also include another dog in the toy play to bring back interest.

Questions
Answered

The more you learn about how enrichment can lead to a happier, healthier dog, the more you'll want to know. The most common questions that pop up relate to why enrichment isn't going as you planned. If you're feeling like your dog isn't enjoying enrichment after getting this far, here are some ways to assess and adapt your enrichment routines for your pup.

How can I make sure my dog is challenged but not frustrated by an enrichment activity?

While we all want to level up our dogs' enrichment once they master something, we must realize that this can only go so far. We don't want to take enrichment games to a place where our dogs are beyond frustrated and cannot complete the game or activity. The second our dogs get frustrated, it negates the purpose of enrichment altogether.

Enrichment should always be achievable and enjoyable. This is why it's so important to know some basic canine body language signals to keep an eye out for signs of frustration. Here are some cues to check on while your dog is engaged in enrichment.

POSITIVE:

- **Exaggerated movements and gestures.** Loose, "goofy" body language during games and activities is a good sign that your dog is having fun. When you spot playful hops and gestures, a loose forehead, and relaxed ears, consider the reaction positive.

- **Shake off and return.** In the wise words of Taylor Swift, sometimes we just have to shake it off—and so do our dogs! If you see your dog shake off and return to the game, this move is a good indicator that they're simply shaking off the stimulation and coming back for more.

- **Play bows.** These are good indicators that your dog is engaging in positive play.

NEGATIVE:

- **Hyperfixation.** While we want our dogs to be engaged in enrichment activities, we don't want them to hyperfixate to the point that they become consumed by something. An example of this is fetch obsession.

- **Whining, crying, or barking excessively.** While a bark or a whine here and there isn't cause for concern, whining, crying, and barking excessively at a toy or game can be an indicator of frustration. If your dog is barking excessively, offer them some help as needed.

- **Lip licking, cowering, and whale eye (the canine equivalent of side-eye).** These three cues are often signs of stress in our canine counterparts. If your dog shows you these signals, try to find the reason the activity is causing stress. Modify accordingly.

Can puppies engage in enrichment?

Yes! The main goal of enrichment is to nurture physical and psychological health, so enrichment is definitely something to begin thinking about as soon as you welcome a puppy into your home. The right type of enrichment can expose your puppy to new sights, sounds, and experiences in a safe and controlled way.

How to start? Let's break it down with the PUPPY acronym.

P — Placement. Make sure the enrichment item or game is placed properly to set your pup up for success. For example, place a clunky feeder toy on a mat or carpet if your puppy is a bit wary of tile or wood floors. Keep games and activities within reach, on even ground.

U — Understanding. Watch and try to recognize your puppy's body language. Understanding their signals will help you avoid a frustrated, overstimulated puppy.

P — Piece of cake. Start with simple games and only advance once your pup gains confidence.

P — Positive. Positive associations with enrichment games and desired play behaviors keep your puppy engaged and excited. See your pup playing positively with a game or puzzle? Reward them with praise and treats.

Y — You. As your pup's guide to the world, you can always offer help and modify games and activities as needed. Plus, interactive play with your puppy can only help strengthen your bond. Never hesitate to join in the fun!

How can I help my nervous dog with enrichment?

Nervous dogs can benefit from enrichment just as much as more confident dogs. In fact, you can use enrichment to create distraction and even positive associations in stressful situations. Just go slowly and always watch for the feedback your dog is giving you.

Allow Time to Decompress

While it can be exciting to offer your nervous dog enrichment, slow and steady wins the race. Allow your dog time to decompress before the activity if their enrichment introduces a new element—the setting or the toy, for example. Then also allow time for your dog to decompress and relax post-enrichment. Think of this as pre- and post-enrichment care. Nervous dogs benefit from transitions.

Start Simple

Start enrichment at the most simple, basic level to allow room for easy "wins." These little wins solidify positive experiences and can help your dog gain confidence. I usually recommend basic snuffle mats, snuffle towels, or scatter feeding to start. If your dog is struggling to obtain treats, sprinkle some free treats above the game and offer praise when they find them on their own. I often call this "making it rain!"

Be Mindful of Noise

For fearful dogs, loud noises can be extremely overwhelming. Try setting up enrichment on a mat and/or rug to muffle loud sounds, or try quiet enrichment options that don't clang, bang, or smash into things. For example, try the soft interactive Planet Dog Orbee Tuff Snoop instead of the clunky KONG Wobbler. While both toys mimic the same type of foraging behavior, the Snoop's material makes it quieter to interact with.

Skip Crazy Movements

While many dogs love small skittery movements, others will head for the hills if they see something moving too quickly. Try starting with calmer toys and activities with little or no movement, such as lick mats or snuffle mats (especially with a suction cup holding the mat in place). Even a basic stuffed KONG could work, just not a KONG Treat Spinner. When your dog is ready, gradually transition to toys with small, anticipated movements.

Encourage and Provide Help

The key to positive enrichment is positive engagement. Never be afraid to offer lots of praise and help when needed. For some dogs, this means creating a positive association around a toy before it's used for the first time. Providing help and setting your dog up for success can make them feel more comfortable navigating a new activity.

Sometimes getting down on their level and showing them how something works is a good place to start.

Follow Your Dog's Lead and Modify Accordingly

Enrichment isn't a linear experience, and it doesn't need to be difficult to be effective. Contrary to popular belief, small, low-key activities are often just as enjoyable for our furry friends. Start small and increase the challenge when (and if) your dog is ready for more. If something is too hard, never hesitate to take it down a notch so that your dog can enjoy it without frustration.

Remember: Enrichment is supposed to be *enjoyable*.

What are the best starter enrichment toys if I can only invest in a few?

With so many enrichment toys available to purchase, it can be overwhelming to narrow down the choices. The easiest way to start is to select toys that hit different enrichment categories that appeal to a wide variety of dogs: foraging, interactive, and physical play. This could be, for example, a snuffle mat (for foraging), a KONG Wobbler (interactive), and a flirt pole (for physical play). Watch your dog's reaction to these before you make your next enrichment purchase. The more your dog engages in enrichment activities, the clearer it will become to see what your dog enjoys the most. But variety is always good too.

Do colors matter when selecting enrichment toys?

Despite the old myths, dogs' vision isn't limited to black and white. They can actually see some colors although not as many as humans can. Dogs are red-green color-blind, which means they can only see shades of blue and yellow. Try picking out toys that are blue or yellow and see how your pup reacts to them. You may notice a difference in their interaction with the toys, indicating that the color of the toy is significant in their visual perception.

I tried stuffing feeder toys for my dog, but he doesn't seem motivated by them. What am I doing wrong?

The two most common reasons that dogs walk away from feeder toys:

Not the right recipe. Are you using ingredients your dog genuinely enjoys? Take a muffin tin and place various dog-safe chopped ingredients in each cup space. Place the tin in front of your dog. What does he go for first? What does he not touch at all? This can be great information to have when stuffing feeder toys.

Not food-motivated. Certain dogs are simply not food-motivated, and enrichment toy stuffing is not as likely to get them going as much as a flirt pole or ball pit. Some dogs prefer play or sensory enrichment over food enrichment, and that's okay!

My dog starts devouring but then leaves everything at the bottom of their feeder toy. What's going on?

Most of the time this is due to improper sizing. To find out if this is a size issue and not your dog losing interest, put a high-value treat (your dog's absolute favorite thing—think cooked chicken or cheddar cheese) at the very bottom of the toy and stuff the rest. If your dog leaves this high-value treat at the base, consider sizing down. Sizing guides on feeder toy packaging or websites can guide you.

Our newly adopted dog doesn't seem interested in *any* enrichment toy I provide. What's going on?

When your dog is new to the household, enrichment may not seem interesting because everything around them is new and exciting. In these situations, we often see something called feigned indifference. This is when the dog in front of you acts like they don't care about a toy or a game because of their current surroundings. Example: Your dog might go crazy for a certain ball or plush but then act indifferent when there are visitors around, or when you're visiting a different house. In these scenarios, the surroundings might be too interesting for your dog to ignore (making the surroundings higher value than the toy).

Allow the dog some time to decompress

in their new space or situation, and try again when they're a bit more settled. I know that it can be exciting to have a new dog in the home, and many people want to do "all of the things" right away. Don't get discouraged; just give your new companion some time to adjust.

Can my dog with physical challenges enjoy enrichment?

If your dog has a disability, they can still benefit from enrichment. In fact, a dog with physical challenges may need the outlet and decompression all the more. Talk with your vet or a trainer about how to modify enrichment activities for their specific needs, and always offer help when needed.

Some examples of modifying an activity for a dog with a challenge include:

Megaesophagus: Most dogs with megaesophagus must eat sitting up so that gravity can help at mealtime. You can adapt a food enrichment activity by putting wet food on a lick mat and then duct-taping the mat to a front-facing, tall surface to accommodate vertical enjoyment at mealtimes.

Blindness: Tailor your enrichment to the other senses at your dog's disposal, which may be quite strong to accommodate for the vision loss. Design activities that stimulate sound, touch, taste, and smell. For example, your dog may not enjoy a flirt pole but may go crazy for a snuffle mat. No one enrichment is better than another; it all depends on the dog in front of you!

Paralysis: Aim for activities that are best

achieved with minimal to no movement. Think: snuffle mats, lick mats, and frozen stuffable feeder toys contained inside a bowl so that they can't roll away.

Will enrichment cure my dog's naughty behavior?

Oftentimes, pet owners assume that providing their dog with plenty of enrichment activities is the key to solving any and all problematic behavior their pet may exhibit. While it's true that enrichment can have an extremely positive effect on your dog's behavior, it should not be seen as an overnight, once-and-done solution to all behavioral issues.

Enrichment activities are meant to meet your dog's innate needs and channel their

energy in positive ways. However, it is crucial to remember that they are just one piece of the puzzle when it comes to responsible pet ownership. Proper training, a healthy diet, adequate socialization, and a comfortable living environment all play a critical role in your pet's overall well-being.

For example, if your dog is constantly barking at passersby through the window, you cannot simply give them a stuffable feeder toy and expect the behavior to stop overnight. While the toy may serve as a temporary distraction, it is important to address the root cause of the behavior through proper training and socialization.

In essence, enrichment should be viewed as an important tool in your dog ownership tool kit rather than a standalone solution. By utilizing enrichment activities in combination with other responsible pet ownership strategies, you can help ensure that your furry friend is happy, healthy, and well behaved.

How many enrichment activities should I be giving my dog each day?

It would be easy but not accurate to give one magic number. Your enrichment routine will depend largely on the dog in front of you. Consider your dog's breed, age, and personality when thinking about what might be right for them. For example, a 1-year-old border collie and a 10-year-old pug will have very different needs.

My advice: Start slowly and don't overdo it! Even with the best intentions, it's easy to go overboard, which can lead to a very overstimulated dog. Puppies may benefit more from shorter bursts of enrichment activities. Always watch for your dog to give you feedback.

What's the best way to build an enrichment routine at home?

I've found that writing out the benefits of enrichment games, what I've learned from them, and how I can make these activities even more enjoyable for my pets is quite beneficial. I use my notes both for myself and my dogs and also for people who may be looking for advice on what to use with their own dogs at home. These notes are a handy asset that you can look back on and review. One way to approach and organize your note taking: use the 4Ls.

The 4Ls is a retrospective technique through which you can identify what you and your dog loved, loathed, learned, and longed for in an enrichment activity. Essentially, you can use these sheets to reflect on what you took away from activities and games you tried with your dog and how to improve your enrichment game as a team. It's a helpful way of breaking down the thought process.

I've filled out a 4L sheet for you on page 182 as an example. Then on page 183, you'll find a blank sheet that you can copy and use at home.

REVIEWING ACTIVITIES
4Ls Retrospective

Date __3/8/24__

Enrichment type __Kong wobbler__

1. Review and recap the highlights of one specific enrichment activity.

2. Look back on what you did well as a team—both how you introduced the enrichment and how your dog engaged with the activity.

3. Look for areas of improvement.

4. Summarize and plan next steps.

LOVED
What did you and your dog love about the enrichment activity?

Bindi really liked it! Very engaged (especially foraging aspect) and kept coming back for more. I like that it's easy to clean.

Ideas:

LONGED FOR
What did the activity lack? What could make it better?

Bindi seemed a bit nervous when the Wobbler banged into the floor. I also think the banging might annoy my downstairs neighbors. Would love to find a way to make it quieter and last longer.

Ideas:
Next time, place a mat down so that the Wobbler isn't as clunky and loud. Also try filling it up with some wine corks, to make the game last a little longer.

LOATHED
What made things difficult? Was there anything you and your dog didn't like?

Bindi didn't seem to realize when the treats were finished and began trying to chew the top of the Wobbler out of frustration. I don't like the idea of her chewing on this hard plastic, and I also don't want to frustrate her.

Ideas:
Make sure to give the game an end— remove the Wobbler once the treats are finished.

LEARNED
What are the key takeaways?

Bindi enjoys using her nose and foraging instincts with this toy. Would be good to look for more variations - something a little quieter. I will always need to supervise her with this toy so she doesn't chew the top.

Ideas:

	Notes from 4Ls	Action(s) to Take	Circle Back	Additional Notes
AMPLIFY (LOVED)	Bindi enjoyed the Kong Wobbler.	Add this into our enrichment routine.	She still seems to love it— even after a month of use!	
ADD (LONGED FOR)	I wish the game was a little quieter.	Find ways to make it less noisy; check out other enrichment items that may be a better fit for quieter foraging.	I purchased the Planet Dog Snoop—less noisy but offers the same foraging aspect.	
REMOVE (LOATHED)	We could have done without Bindi chewing the top.	Always remove after play— don't leave the Wobbler out.	No mishaps since removing the toy after use.	
TRY (LEARNED)	Bindi really likes interactive foraging games.	Find more ways to incorporate foraging behaviors into other games and activities.	She's really happy and engaged with any new foraging activities I try. I've noticed that she is less destructive around the house as a result!	

REVIEWING ACTIVITIES
4Ls Retrospective

Date _____

Enrichment type _____

1. Review and recap the highlights of one specific enrichment activity.

2. Look back on what you did well as a team—both how you introduced the enrichment and how your dog engaged with the activity.

3. Look for areas of improvement.

4. Summarize and plan next steps.

LOVED

What did you and your dog love about the enrichment activity?

Ideas:

LONGED FOR

What did the activity lack? What could make it better?

Ideas:

LOATHED

What made things difficult? Was there anything you and your dog didn't like?

Ideas:

LEARNED

What are the key takeaways?

Ideas:

	Notes from 4Ls	Action(s) to Take	Circle Back	Additional Notes
AMPLIFY (LOVED)				
ADD (LONGED FOR)				
REMOVE (LOATHED)				
TRY (LEARNED)				

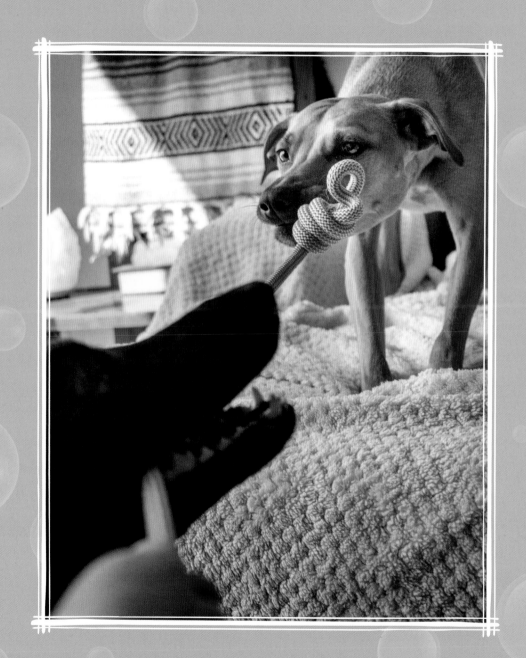

Enrichment Match Game

With so many options for canine enrichment, it can be difficult to choose. Know this: The best enrichment activities are the ones that meet your dog's unique needs and your personal situation. To help you zero in on the choices that are right for you and your dog, turn to the at-a-glance A-to-Z chart in this chapter. Identify what factors are important to you and desirable to your dog, then look for the activities that check the boxes.

	Indoor	Outdoor	Good for Puppies	Good for Older Dogs	Good for All Ages	Good for Sensitive Dogs	Good for You Too	Quick Setup	Uses Recycled Items	
Backyard Fishing 103		X								
Bathing Beauty 126	X									
Bubble Mania 105	X	X	X					X		
Canine Birthday Cake 78	X		X	X	X					
Canine TV 155	X		X	X	X	X		X		
Chicken Bone Broth 72	X		X	X	X	X	X			
Chomp & Chase 91	X		X					X		
Crinkle Ball 96	X		X						X	
Dig Pit (Permanent) 100		X								
Dig Pit (Temporary) 99		X								
Dissecting Diversion 95	X								X	
Doggy Day Out 130		X					X			
Edible Shreddables 85	X									
Egg-cellent Carton Game 43	X	X			X			X	X	
Errand Exploration 133		X								
Firework Calm 129	X					X				
Flirt Pole Play 89		X								
Frozen Layered Cake 81	X	X	X	X	X					

THE HAPPIEST DOG ON THE BLOCK

Works Well for Multiple Dogs	Soothing	Bond Building	Food Motivation	Nonfood Enrichment	Socialization	Cognitive Challenge	Emphasis on Choice	Sensory Experience	Energy Outlet	Shredding Outlet	Digging Outlet	Water Play
			X	X		X		X				X
	X	X	X									X
X				X				X	X			
			X	X				X				
X	X			X				X				
			X									
			X			X		X	X			
			X	X		X		X	X	X		
				X				X	X		X	
				X				X	X		X	
				X				X			X	
		X	X	X	X	X	X	X	X		X	X
			X					X		X		
	X		X			X		X		X		
		X	X		X	X		X				
	X	X	X									
		X		X		X			X			
		X	X					X				

	Indoor	Outdoor	Good for Puppies	Good for Older Dogs	Good for All Ages	Good for Sensitive Dogs	Good for You Too	Quick Setup	Uses Recycled Items
Goal Getters 124	X	X					X		
Gopher Hole 93	X								X
Herding Ball Play 109		X							
Hide-and-Treat Tin 53	X		X						X
High Five 115	X	X	X	X	X				
Homebody Beats 156	X		X	X	X	X			
Muffin Lick Tin 83	X		X	X	X				
Paper Tube Snuffler 45	X								X
Party Cup Scent Seek 38	X	X							
PB & Banana Smoothie Mat 67	X		X	X	X				
Pooch Ball Pit 163		X	X						
Pup Pizza Party 75	X		X	X	X		X		
Pup Playdate 137		X							
Pupkin Spice Cup 61	X				X	X	X		X
Pupper-mint Stuffer 62	X				X	X			
Pupsicles 71		X	X	X	X				
Scatter Feeding 37		X			X	X		X	
Scentsory Box 40	X	X	X	X	X				X

THE HAPPIEST DOG ON THE BLOCK

Works Well for Multiple Dogs	Soothing	Bond Building	Food Motivation	Nonfood Enrichment	Socialization	Cognitive Challenge	Emphasis on Choice	Sensory Experience	Energy Outlet	Shredding Outlet	Digging Outlet	Water Play
		X	X	X	X	X			X			
				X		X						
				X		X			X			
			X			X	X	X		X		
		X		X		X						
X	X			X				X				
	X		X					X				
			X			X		X		X		
			X			X						
	X			X				X				
X				X	X			X	X			
X				X				X				
X				X	X	X			X			
				X				X				
		X	X					X				
			X					X				
			X			X		X				
				X		X		X				

	Indoor	Outdoor	Good for Puppies	Good for Older Dogs	Good for All Ages	Good for Sensitive Dogs	Good for You Too	Quick Setup	Uses Recycled Items	
Sensory Pathway 147	X	X	X							
Sensory Yard 148		X			X		X			
Sniffari Adventure 35		X					X			
Sniffy Wall 142		X					X			
Snuffle Cinnamon Buns 47	X				X					
Snuffle Snack Break 25	X		X	X	X	X		X		
Squeak & Seek 107	X	X						X		
Stingray Snuffle Puzzle 27	X		X	X	X	X			X	
Sunshine Sounds 159		X					X			
Suite Choices 160	X		X	X	X	X		X		
Tail-Wagging Breakfast 65	X									
Touch Targeting 119	X	X			X	X				
Towel Tornado 31	X				X			X	X	
Toy Bin Bonanza 165	X				X			X	X	
Treat Tumblers 51	X		X	X	X			X	X	
TTouch Ear Slides 122	X	X	X	X	X	X		X		
Tug of Play 121	X	X	X					X		
Window Watching 145	X			X	X					

Works Well for Multiple Dogs	Soothing	Bond Building	Food Motivation	Nonfood Enrichment	Socialization	Cognitive Challenge	Emphasis on Choice	Sensory Experience	Energy Outlet	Shredding Outlet	Digging Outlet	Water Play
				X		X	X	X				
X	X			X			X	X			X	X
X		X				X	X	X	X			
	X							X				
			X			X		X				
	X		X			X		X				
		X		X		X						
	X		X			X		X				
	X			X				X				
X	X			X			X					
	X		X					X				
	X	X		X		X						
	X		X			X		X				
					X		X	X				
			X			X		X		X		
	X	X		X								
		X		X					X			
X				X				X